LETITIA BALDRIGE was an assistant to the American ambassador in Paris and Rome, served as Social Secretary to the White House during the Kennedy Administration, was an executive at Tiffany & Co., and now heads her own public relations firm. In this valuable guide, she has expanded and updated the answers to all the questions you need to know about social etiquette and manners, entertaining, holding or attending traditional functions, traveling, gift-giving and more!

Men and women have been searching for new etiquette guidelines. AMY VANDERBILT'S EVERYDAY ETIQUETTE, revised & expanded by Letitia Baldrige, has them in a comprehensive up-to-date and easy-to-use format.

"Covers all aspects of our society ... breaks new ground"

—*Wall Street Journal*

"Provides a ... very complete section on human relationships"

—*N.Y. Post*, Eugenia Sheppard

"Baldrige [is] a superbly energetic amalgam of feminist and Tasteful Lady"

—*Time* magazine

My dearest Bubie,

I'm sending this traditional mother's gift to you with much love and appreciation for the social grace you radiate. I hope it helps in your new responsibilities as a new bride and "coordinater".

Love

Mama

Feb. 1995

Completely Revised and Updated

Amy Vanderbilt's Everyday Etiquette

Letitia Baldrige

BANTAM BOOKS

NEW YORK · TORONTO · LONDON · SYDNEY · AUCKLAND

I have used a variety of names and addresses for the sake of illustration. Any similarity to those of actual people, living or dead, is coincidental.

AMY VANDERBILT'S EVERYDAY ETIQUETTE
*A Bantam Book / published by arrangement with
Doubleday & Co.*

PUBLISHING HISTORY

*Doubleday edition published October 1978
Bantam edition / May 1981*

Serialized in Woman's Day, Ladies Home Journal, The Secretary, East/West Network, Across The Board, The Equitable Life Insurance Magazine *and* Management Quarterly.

Drawing of country-club map by David Perry.

ISBN 0-553-27754-5

Published simultaneously in the United States and Canada

Bantam Books are published by Bantam Books, a division of Bantam Doubleday Dell Publishing Group, Inc. Its trademark, consisting of the words "Bantam Books" and the portrayal of a rooster, is Registered in U.S. Patent and Trademark Office and in other countries. Marca Registrada. Bantam Books, 1540 Broadway, New York, New York 10036.

PRINTED IN THE UNITED STATES OF AMERICA

RAD   19 18 17 16 15

Contents

Party ... The Cocktail Party ... Housewarming and Open House ... The Tea Party ... The Bridge Party ... Family Swimming-Pool Party ... The Picnic ... Being a Host— and Being a Guest—for the Weekend ... The Teen Party ... Table Manners ... How to Eat Certain Foods

Introduction

In October, 1978, my revised and rewritten edition of *The Amy Vanderbilt Complete Book of Etiquette* was published by Doubleday. My life as a former diplomat and now businesswoman, wife and mother, suddenly acquired another dimension: that of *manners observer*. Shortly after the book's publication, *Time* magazine put me on a cover and called me "America's New Social Arbiter," and my postal letter box for questions on manners from the public began to fill to the overflowing. I heard from people who had read the book; I was stopped by people on the street; I was called by business people; I was written to by people from all over the U.S. and Canada who had read my syndicated newspaper column on etiquette. There were questions—and more questions about what people most wanted to know, and about the situations they faced that made them the most uncomfortable. It is these questions, which reflect the small and large problems confronting people in their everyday lives, that form the basis for this book.

If we think we're "doing the right thing," we walk with more ease, we feel better about ourselves, and we interact far more humanely with our fellow men and women. Good manners are, after all, nothing more than a combination of kindness and efficiency. There's nothing old-fashioned about *that*.

Nor, I hope, is there anything old-fashioned about this book, either.

Letitia Baldrige
May 1, 1980

The Importance of Family and Home

Life begins within a family. Manners are taught and character is molded within the family structure. This is how a child learns how to cope with life. Without this knowledge, discipline, and support, the child does not grow easily into a social human being.

Therefore, when two people marry, start a family, and reach toward their individual goals in life, they carry an enormous responsibility toward their joint creation of offspring brought into the world.

It is obvious and visible to everyone that well-mannered parents raise well-mannered children. These are the people, too, who are successful in their careers and in their social lives.

People with good manners care about others. They are happy people.

Baby-sitters

I don't feel at ease when I close the door to our home and leave our baby in the care of a sitter. Is this a normal worry?

You are like many young mothers, so don't worry about it. Just get yourself organized, handle the finding of a well-recommended sitter through a church or a nearby school, check the sitter's references, and give him or her complete, clear instructions. Then you'll be able to close that door without worry.

How does one keep a sitter happy?

Be considerate of the sitter and the sitter will enjoy working for you and taking care of your children. Write specific instructions on the care of the child or children; make the living conditions palatable (give the sitter access to a TV as well as the refrigerator for light snack food); and don't make the sitter do housework if it wasn't part of the original deal.

What kind of instructions should one leave?

Leave emergency numbers, for one thing—where and how to get you by telephone, the number of the children's pediatrician, the address of the emergency entrance of the nearest hospital, the telephone number of the local cab company, and the numbers of the police and fire departments. Leave the name and number of the nearest neighbor who can be relied upon in an emergency, too.

Be sure that the sitter has had a run-through of what steps to take in case of a fire.

Leave a list of what the sitter may eat or drink from the larder.

Make sure the instructions are clear on what the children are to be fed, when is the hour of their bathtime, and also of bedtime. Even a detail such as whether a light is left on and how wide the window is to be left open will affect the child's comfort during the night.

It also helps at the end of the instruction sheet to give the sitter a gentle reminder: "Please wash your dishes and leave the kitchen in order."

I have begun to sit for my mother's friends. I would like my boyfriend to come sit with me when the parents are out, like on Saturday night, until very late. Is it all right to ask if my boyfriend can spend the evening with me, so I won't get lonely?

No, unless you know the family very well, and unless the family, your employers, knows the young man very well, and unless you have express permission.

You are, after all, on a job, being paid, and holding a very serious responsibility. It is not really professional to have a "friend" present to keep you from being bored.

My sitter uses our telephone incessantly. Many times when we are out, I have something to tell her that I forgot—something important. I spend the whole night leaving the party and trying to get through to my house.

I hope you have told her not to use the telephone at all. If she persists, find another sitter. A telephone gabber is not doing her job.

Stepparenting

As a new stepfather to three children, ages seven to sixteen, it's very rocky going. I'm accused by the kids of my new family of loving my own children much more than them; the middle stepchild says I greatly favor the youngest stepchild and am turning her into a spoiled brat; my former wife says I'm neglecting our own children because I see them only one day each weekend (the second day, I'm father to my new family); my new wife says I should pay much more attention to her children; my former wife says my own children are not receiving enough money and that I must be giving more to my stepchildren; my present wife has the same complaint against me, in reverse.

If I listened to everyone, I would never go to work, because I would be playing with children seven days a week. I would also have to rob a bank every month to meet all their financial demands. Any feelings I might have of my own these days have to be totally suppressed.

Your problems are serious and repeated in many stepfamily situations. These are matters that should have been foreseen, and that should have been talked out with all parties concerned *before* your second marriage.

A stepparent should sit down with his or her former spouse and children, and then with the new spouse and children, and talk frankly about the problems that may arise in this second marriage. Even a very young person can comprehend "sacrifice" and "compromise" and "the reality of the situation." They are going to have to live with the latter.

The stepparent should assure his or her own children that parental love will increase, not decrease, with each passing year. The stepparent should assure the new children that love and understanding will grow strong with time; it should be explained that discipline is not a manifestation of criticism and negativism, but rather love and affirmation.

A stepparent would be wise to discuss financial affairs frankly within the new and old families, to explain why certain economies must be enforced.

Money, time, love, and discipline should be meted out equally to the children of both family units.

A stepparent who is honest with both sets of children will be able to keep the communication channels open. Problems should always be expressed, met head-on, and resolved through compromises, because that's what life is all about. It is a process in which respect, and then love, can grow.

My stepson resents my taking so much of his father's time. He claims that before I came into their lives, "we always spent every weekend together."

That happens to be an exaggeration, but nevertheless, the problem is getting serious. The boy is downright hostile to me. My husband and I both work, and I see little enough of the man I married as it is. What should be my response to my stepson?

It will be worth it for your marriage and your future if you try very hard to win that young man over to your side. It won't be a question of a fifty-fifty situation at first. It will have to be all *your* effort. (You can't even remind him of this fact!)

Talk to him frankly in private. Make suggestions for weekend activities all three of you would enjoy. Then take him alone with you on a special expedition. Tell him you care about him very much, and try to make him an integral part of your joint weekends.

Before long, he'll be busy with his own friends on weekends. He won't be so dependent on you both, so don't consider this a never-ending burden. It only *seems* like forever!

My stepchildren were spoiled rotten by their father after their mother's death. I don't know where to begin with their discipline.

When you do begin, start slow and easy. Tell the children that for the sake of everyone's life, discipline must be established in the household, and you are going to have to be the one to do it. Explain that equal amounts of discipline and reward will be your motto; then live up to it. Make a game out of the demerits for bad behavior versus certain rewards for good.

My stepchildren, who live with their mother, want to call me by my first name. They are eight and twelve, and I'm only twenty. Isn't that disrespectful and improper?

It is proper for them to call you by your first name, and certainly not disrespectful. They are trying to find a title for you that does not say "Mother." If a stepchild's mother is dead and the child is quite young, he or she tends to call the stepmother "Mother" for life. Your stepchildren are too old and you are too young for them to call you "Mother"; besides, their own mother is alive.

My former husband never sees our children. He is constantly canceling his weekend plans for them. His "visitation rights" have become a big joke. Since our divorce, both children's grades have fallen noticeably. It's from heartbreak, I'm convinced.

Have a teacher or a counselor from the school call your husband and ask him to come in for an appointment. If that counselor explains the children are upset by not seeing him when they expect to, perhaps his habits will change. There might be a member of his family—a brother or sister—whom he respects and who could represent the children's interests in making him see how destructive he is.

The Adopted Child

What kind of gesture should we make toward our friends' newly adopted child?

It is nice to send the newly arrived adopted child a present. If it's a small baby, a woman friend might hold a shower for the mother, as for any new arrival. In sending an engraved gift, use the child's actual birthdate, not his adoption date. A warm letter congratulating the new parents on the arrival of the child will be much appreciated, too.

What terminology is used in talking about an adopted child?

In speaking of the original parents, one should not use terms like "the real mother" or "the true father," but rather "birth parents," "biological parents," and "bio-parents." The child should be referred to as their "biological child."

When talking with the adoptive parents, it is important to treat the adopted child within the normal context of the family—no singling out, and no treatment as though he or she were an oddity.

If your child asks you about another adopted child, how should you explain it?

Answer your child succinctly, but do not dwell on the subject. Explain adoption so that your child will know it is an act of love, not an unusual thing. Show your child that an adopted child is loved and cared for by his new "real parents" in the very same way your own child is loved and cared for.

Problems with In-laws and Aged Parents

My mother-in-law constantly interferes with our lives every time she comes to our home. My wife resents it as much as I do. She drops in whenever she feels like it, including on the weekends, our only time to relax together. Is there a way of being firm, polite, and kind at the same time?

Yes. Some evening when everyone is relaxed, let your wife start off by saying to her mother that you would both feel better if you could have your weekends to yourselves. Explain that you wish to see her "often," but on a regularly scheduled basis, so that she won't be "dropping in" all the time. She's bound to be offended, but if you show her that you both love her and enjoy her visits, but just want to be able to plan on your own social schedule—in order to give her more time and attention when she *does* come to see you—she might be able to see it your way. Handle the conversation gently. It's important that you make her go through this difficult period, for your own sakes.

I have always fed my son and only child nutritious meals. He is now married and ill-nourished. His wife never cooks for him. He's living out of cans, and I think it is perfectly terrible. I think it's time I said something to him and his wife, don't you?

No. It's your son's problem and your son's stomach. Don't interfere and upset that marriage. It's up to your son to arrange to eat better food in his own home. It might require his learning how to cook himself!

We have finally persuaded my mother-in-law to enter a nursing home. Is there any one thing we should be doing to make her stay there a pleasant one?

No, not just one thing. There are many things to be done to keep her interested in the world, to make her feel she is still loved, not abandoned, still a part of the family.

Visit her *often* and *regularly*. If she is far away, write her constantly, and have your children follow suit. Send her small inexpensive gifts—things like a nice cake of soap, a box of notepaper. Send her your magazines when you have read them. Give her a gift subscription to her local newspaper.

If your mother-in-law is capable of handling her own affairs, let her pay her own bills and use her own checking account. Even if her income is very small, give her the self-respect of managing it herself, if she is able to.

My wife's father is coming to live with us. I want this experience to be as pleasant as possible for him, for my wife, and for the rest of the family. Are there any guaranteed secrets of making a grandparent-in-residence a successful operation?

The joy of having a grandparent at home can be one of the greatest pluses in all your lives, particularly those of your children. A grandparent *always* has time for a child, and often can console an unhappy child better than anyone else. A grandparent, in the wisdom of experience, can stretch a child's horizons for him, open up new worlds to explore and appreciate.

Give your father-in-law his own room, with some of his own furnishings in it (particularly things like pictures and bibelots). His own TV or radio is important, if that can be arranged. Make the room bright and cheerful—perhaps a coat of paint is all that is necessary.

Write down the list of "family rules" that everyone has to live by, whether it concerns locking the door at night or putting all dishes, nicely rinsed, into the dishwasher before leaving the kitchen. Give him some responsibility, so that he will feel useful to the family: perhaps the care and feeding (and extra loving) of the family dog, or doing the marketing, or tending to the little garden in back. Perhaps he could be made vice-president in charge of getting the children up, fed, and off to school in the morning.

Make him feel loved and needed. Teach your children to respect his privacy, and at the same time make sure he understands that you wish your own privacy respected.

It should be a happy, wonderful experience.

Children's Manners

How do you teach a child good household manners, especially things like picking up the bedroom and not leaving the bathroom in a mess?

As soon as a child can read, post a gentle reminder on a bulletin board or a central place, detailing the things you have been teaching him during these early years—a litany of "do this" and "don't do that." (Be sure there are many more "dos" than "don'ts.")

Make your behavior list fun. Draw some appropriately happy or sad faces around it, or paste some cut-out figures on the chart. Give the child a paste-on gold star for "a specially good week" as a reward symbol.

Don't expect an overnight miracle, but a child can learn to see the logic in good manners and having consideration for others. It means better living for everyone in the house, and a young child is often more logical than his parents!

As soon as your child develops good self-discipline and a sense of "home manners," you can throw away the list of dos and don'ts. It won't be needed anymore.

We have a two-year-old. I've heard one of the most important things in the world is to teach him respect for authority. Will you explain exactly what that implies, and how one instills it in a young mind?

It *is* the most important lesson for a member of any society to learn. Without it, a society becomes a state of chaos, self-destructing. Your two-year-old is learning a respect for authority when he or she stops pursuing a course of action to which you have said a firm no. On the bus, the child learns to obey the bus driver, who is in command. In Sunday-school the teacher is a voice of authority, and his day-school teacher is another one.

A child learns to respect the clergyman, the policeman, the fireman, and the salesman in the store. He learns that when he is in someone else's domain, he must obey that person's rules just as he obeys his own parents in their home.

He also learns that authority over him can be passed from one person to another—such as when his parents go out in the evening and tell him to obey the baby-sitter and "be a good boy."

What should a parent teach a child on the subject of nicely greeting one's adult friends? I mean, if I'm walking down the street with my daughter Sarah, what should she do when I run into my friend Sue Johnson?

The first step is yours. You should introduce your daughter *to* the older person. You might say, "Sue, this is my daughter Sarah. Sarah, you remember Mrs. Johnson."

Sarah should then extend her hand and shake Mrs. Johnson's as she says, "Hello, Mrs. Johnson."

If you stand there chatting for quite a while, when you take your leave, Sarah should once again put out her hand and say, "Good-bye, Mrs. Johnson."

What should my children do when an adult friend comes into a room at home where the children are studying, playing, or watching TV?

When an adult from the outside enters that room for the first time that day, each child should rise to a standing position (from the floor, from the sofa, wherever) and extend his or her hand for a handshake. If he knows the adult, he would say, "Hello, Mr. Gates." If he doesn't know the adult, he does not shake his hand, but gives him as cheery a smile of welcome as he can muster. "Hello, I'm Jeremy Williams," he should explain to the adult. The adult will then explain who he or she is.

How do you teach a child to say thank-you properly?

If you care enough to teach him, he'll learn. It's the parents who don't care enough who fall down on the job of teaching their children one of the most important responsibilities of life: knowing when and how to say thanks.

A baby learns about this part of manners when his or her mother smiles and says with exaggeration, "Oh, thank you *very* much," when the baby hands over something. The baby comes to know that "Thank you" is an automatic response to something nice the baby does in reference to that person. The phrase is learned simultaneously with another very important word in our vocabulary, "Please."

By the time the baby is three, he or she should say "Thank you" without being prompted (too much) when handed a toy or a gift. The parents in the meantime should have been sending thank-you notes on the child's behalf for every party attended and every present given by a relative or friend.

Soon a child will want to write his or her own thank-you notes. Give your child some amusing stationery, sit him down, give him some parental guidance about the text, and write the envelope for him, so the postman can read it easily. "Thank you for the party" sandwiched in between "Dear Jimmy" and "Love, Ellen" is sufficient when a child learns to write.

As an acknowledgment of a gift: "Thank you for my present" is enough text in the early years. By the fourth grade, the letters become more elaborate: "Thank you for having me to the party. Your mother makes good cake, and I liked the water-pistol fight." A thank-you for a gift also takes on a more personal touch, as the child learns to add details: "Thank you for my Christmas present. I have named the doll Clara Anne, and she is a good girl. I give her vitamin pills every day, too, so she won't have colds this winter."

What kind of host is a young child expected to be at his or her own birthday party?

A good one. He or she should be sympathetic and try to help when a guest is upset for some reason (a birthday guest may be upset for any number of reasons: he may not like the present he brought ... she may have had her frosting stolen ... he may not have won any game prize ... another guest may have been mean to her).

A birthday host is supposed to thank each child for every present received, and not let the guest know he or she already has that present. A host is not supposed to keep any game prize he or she may win at the party. A host says good-bye to each guest at the end. If the guest doesn't say "thank you," the host can practice one-upmanship with that guest by saying, "Thank you for coming to my party!"

Our young son sounds like someone from the Stone Age when he answers the telephone. The caller receives a series of grunts, "yehs" and "dunnos." Is there any way to train him to answer the telephone in a civilized way?

Tape him answering a call and taking a message when he is unaware of it. When you play it back for him, he will probably be surprised at the way he sounds. Don't make fun of him, but point out that maybe he himself would like to give a better impression of himself.

Post by the telephone a simple scenario of sentences and phrases used in an average call:

"Hello."

"No, I'm sorry, my mother can't come to the telephone right now." (She's in the bathtub, but you don't give that information.)

"Who's calling, please?"

"How is that spelled, please?"

"And the number?" (Repeats number as written, so that if there is an error, it will be corrected.)

"Fine, I'll have my mother call you as soon as possible."
"Thank you, good-bye."

Our oldest girl is driving the entire family to insanity. She is constantly on the phone. Her friends are always calling her, and at times very inconvenient to our family. She has been pressing us for her own telephone line for two years now, saying that would make the problem evaporate. We have refused, for economic and other reasons. What would you do?

First of all, I would lay down the law about the time she is permitted exclusive use of the family telephone. Give her one to two hours' total time in which the instrument is hers to make or receive calls. She should inform her friends of your edict. That should stop any calls coming when you're making breakfast or have gone to bed.

Inform her that she may have her own telephone line *if* she pays for the entire installation and monthly charges out of her own savings and future earnings. Tell her that when her private phone rings and she is out, no one will go into her room to answer it. (These codicils may make her reconsider her desire to have her own line.)

I'm embarrassed when our small children notice someone who is handicapped or who has a special problem. If they see someone who is very fat or very thin, someone who is wearing a patch over an eye or has leg braces, they inevitably point, stare, discuss, and giggle about that person. What should I do about it?

Whisper that they should be quiet, not stare but look away at once. Then say, "I'll explain it to you later."

At home, don't forget to explain it to them, so they'll understand that just because the person they saw was somewhat different from what they are used to, it does not mean that that person does not have the same intellect, emotions, and feelings as they do. Show them how basically unkind it is to draw attention to others. Explain that the person can't help being that way, and discuss how courageous a blind man is, for example, to board the bus with his dog. Sympathize with the extremely heavy woman—how difficult life must be for her. Mention how terribly hard life would be if one couldn't hear.

Explain that there are many kinds and degrees of handicaps and that children should always be sympathetic to someone with these problems, but also realize that they have normal minds and feelings.

The best way to teach your child how to view people with special problems is to show consideration yourself. When you see someone in difficulty on the bus, get up quickly and help that person into your seat. That is the best lesson of all for your child to witness.

We watch our language very carefully at home, even though I know a lot of parents who don't. We send our children to good schools, at a financial sacrifice. Yet, since the beginning of the fourth grade, our children have come home using foul language that they obviously picked up at school. How is a parent supposed to handle this?

Children pick up "street talk" with the greatest of ease. It's a very contagious disease. A parent should react with initial displeasure, maybe even a little shock, but then dismiss it with a casual "Did you really know what you just said? Did you understand that word? I thought not. Well, I suggest that until you understand a word, you should not use it. Besides, it makes you look very unattractive, coming from your mouth."

If a young child's language becomes increasingly full of obscenities, it may be a sign of a disturbed child. Professional help should be sought.

Bad language often becomes ingrained in a teenager, because of peer pressure. Some teenagers think obscenities are a way of sounding adult and sophisticated. When they hold down jobs, they might be fired for talking that way—certainly in a business office they will be—and that fact of life is a very sobering one.

When a child grows into adolescence and then learns that bad language is a sign of immaturity, not adult suavity, he or she usually drops the habit.

Allowances

We have three children, and I feel each should receive a standard allowance that goes up according to age. My husband feels an allowance should always be earned. Are there any definite guidelines to follow or is there no established philosophy concerning a child's allowance?

Each family sets its own rules for allowances, based on what the peer group is receiving (if they can afford it). The guidelines are based on common sense.

Each child should have some chores at home which are part of his regular contribution to the functioning of family life. These tasks are *not* paid employment, nor should they have anything to do with an allowance.

If you can afford an allowance for your children, find out what the average sum is in each child's grade. This allowance should be considered untouchable and a right (again, unless failing family finances rule otherwise).

Realistic teaching can help a child understand how to handle money. A young child should be taught how money "grows in a savings account." He should be taught to save a portion of the allowance for something every week that is attainable (a baseball mitt rather than a bicycle; a bowl with two goldfish rather than an illuminated, electrified aquarium).

Once the allowance is given over, the parents should only suggest how to spend it when asked. Parents should never ridicule a frivolous purchase or compare one child's spending habits with another's in the family.

Teen Manners

If you were asked to write a "Checklist of Good Manners for Young People," what would you include?

Many of the items on my list were on George Washington's list of fifty-four maxims, written by him when he was just sixteen!

MANNERS CHECKLIST

Always say *thank-you, excuse me,* and *please* when you have been done a favor or when you are apologizing.

Write a note to someone you love who has received good news—or to someone you love who has received bad news.

Invite your least popular classmate to your party, simply because that person is probably only rarely invited anywhere, and it would mean so much.

Be a bathroom-manners expert—which means you are meticulous in tidying up and you are considerate of others who use the bathroom.

Be creative for a friend who is sick at home or in the hospital.

Keep down your noise level when it could disturb others nearby.

Don't blow bubblegum bubbles in others' faces; don't crack gum when anyone else will hear it.

Always knock and ask permission before entering someone's room.

Always RSVP promptly to every invitation you receive.

When your parents ask you to do something, do it cheerfully and well—the tasks are easier and accomplished faster that way.

Return anything borrowed on time, and in good condition.

Be on time for appointments; leave on time, too, for nothing is more boring than someone who overstays his welcome.

Learn how to pay compliments. Start with the members of your family, and you will find it will become easier later in life to compliment others. It's a great asset.

Go upstairs and downstairs quietly, not like a lumbering elephant.

Open and shut doors softly.

Don't "leave it for the next person" when an unpleasant task presents itself, whether it's cleaning out the lint trap in the clothes dryer or cleaning up the dog's mess on the rug.

Obey all signs. They have a purpose.

Don't put your feet upon the furniture. Feet do not enhance the look of the desk or the table.

Give up your seat on public transport to someone who needs it more than you do.

Be a good volunteer. Help out when there's a need—whether it's your school, church, club, or any group that could use your time, your brains, and/or your brawn.

Don't spit, pick your teeth, fiddle with your nails, or comb your hair in public. Girls should never apply makeup in front of others.

Treat books with the greatest respect. Treat public property the same way, and that means no graffiti.

Never cheat on your place in line.

When you dial a wrong number, say, "I'm sorry, excuse me"—instead of slamming down the receiver in the other person's ear.

Drive your car carefully, not only out of consideration for others but also to save lives. The same holds true of motorcycles, skateboards, and roller skates!

Show respect to anyone in authority, from your parents to your bus driver.

How do you train kids not to shout and scream so much when they're in public vehicles? On crowded streets? On beaches and in parks when people are trying to rest? At home when they turn up the sound system and interfere with the peace of the entire neighborhood?

Teenagers have a natural ebullience that seems to burst out of them when they're away from a structured period, such as the hours spent in school.

Kindness--not hostility or sarcasm—always works best to make a noisy teenager realize he or she is adversely affecting the peace and comfort of others Yelling at someone who is making too much noise will goad that person to increase the volume Begin in a calm, cool, soothing voice, by asking "Please, would you be kind enough to lower the noise level for the sake of the rest of us?"

Appalling noise pollution is everywhere these days—in the streets, in public transport, on the beaches—because kids keep their transistors turned up high with their terrible rock music. I find even my own kids are guilty. What's the remedy?

Try giving your own child some of his own medicine. Wait until he or she is resting, studying, or sleeping. Find a radio station playing the kind of music your child hates (probably the "I Love You Truly" kind), turn the radio up to an ear-splitting volume, and leave it at his door. He or she just might get the message.

Young Person's Table Manners

By the time my child is entering high school, what should he know about table manners?

By the time he is a high-school freshman, his table manners should be almost as polished as when he is an adult. The only difference is that he will know when he is older how to attack an artichoke properly; eat asparagus with his fingers, dipping it into the sauce; eat snails in metal holders and sip their garlicky sauce; and polish off a boiled lobster, aided by an oyster pick and a nutcracker. Or perhaps he won't ever have to know those things.

By the time he's fourteen, he should know that one takes small bites so the mouth won't be full and wipes the mouth with a napkin after drinking or taking a messy bit of any food. He knows that one doesn't talk with the mouth full, eat chicken with the fingers at an indoor dinner party with adults, or use a toothpick at table.

At a buffet party, the young teenager should know that in respect to his elders, he goes to the end of the food line and lets the adults go first. He should not sit down at the table until the adults who will sit at his table have taken their places.

He should know enough not to tilt back in his chair, but to sit up straight (in the interest of preserving good chairs as well as his spine). He controls his nervous habits now, like finger-drumming on the table.

He now knows how to unfold his napkin properly on his lap—half fold if it's an oversized dinner napkin, completely unfolded if it's a smaller-sized luncheon napkin. At the end of the meal, when everyone gets up to leave the table, then and only then does he neatly fold it again and place it on top of the table.

He knows by now to take small, not pig-sized portions of his favorite foods—knowing (well, at least hoping) that the platter will be passed to him again or that he will be invited to step up to the serving table again with his plate.

If someone serves him from a large serving platter, he knows how to replace the serving fork and spoon side by side on the platter or in the bowl, for the convenience of the next person to be served, and that if he should let the serving spoon fall into the gravy or sauce, he will clean the handle with his napkin, so that the next person won't have to cope with *his* mistake.

He knows that if his host has started, he may eat also, but that at a big party, if there are many to be served, and the food is hot, he should begin to eat even before everyone is served.

If he dislikes what is served, he is diplomatic enough to pretend to eat a bit so as not to embarrass his host. He is now grown-up enough to refrain from saying "I hate fish" or "I can't eat this stuff."

He knows that one tilts a soup bowl away from oneself and spoons the remaining liquid with a flourish of the utensil away from oneself, instead of toward oneself. He knows that one has to practice eating soup silently, too. "Slurping is something only kids do." He even knows that the soup spoon is not placed at rest in the cup or bowl, but on the saucer beneath.

He knows that he selects his eating utensils from the outside toward the middle (where the plate is). In other words, for the first course, he chooses the outermost fork or spoon, and works his way inward for the next course.

He doesn't reach across the table for the salt and pepper. He waits for a moment when he's not interrupting someone's conversation, and then asks the person nearest the spices to hand them to him. He knows not to pour salt and pepper on his food before tasting it.

He also knows not to ask the host for catsup or mustard to put on the meat dish, even if he thinks it would taste better.

As he eats, he keeps his elbows close to his body, so as not to hit a neighbor in the ribs. He has probably been raised to eat American-style (cutting with the fork in the left hand, the knife in the right, then laying down the knife and transferring the fork to the right hand for eating purposes). He may switch to the continental style, particularly if he studies or travels abroad. (In the latter style, the fork stays in the left hand, the knife in the right.)

If he is having dinner in a fancy restaurant or hotel, he might be served a finger bowl on a doily on a plate. He should put the doily to the upper left of his plate, and then place the finger bowl upon it. (He should not, as my nine-year-old daughter did at the Williamsburg Inn, drink from it, as from a glass of water!) His empty plate is now ready to receive dessert. After dessert, he will dip the tips of his fingers into the bowl to rinse them, and then wipe his fingers dry on his napkin. (When he first uses the finger bowl, he may feel a little foolish, but if he knows everyone did the first time, it's not so bad.)

Please settle a table-manners argument. My friend says it is considered polite to leave a little bit of food on one's plate. I was always taught to clean my plate by my parents. Who's right?

Traditionally, the school of clean-your-plate has alternated with the school of leave-a-little. I personally feel that in our economy, with the cost of food, one should eat every bit of food one takes. The answer is to take the right-size portion—not too much food.

Our fourteen-year-old son wants to begin dating. He is shy and awkward, an only child, and we ourselves are confused about the mores of today's dating. How can we help him launch forth into the dating world?

The first thing to master is how to make the date in the first place. Sometimes asking a girl for a date on the telephone is easier for a young man than in a face-to-face meeting.

Before he makes that call, he should jot down on a piece of paper all the information he must communicate, so that no important details will be omitted: the occasion, where is it, when is it, what will everyone be wearing, is a meal included, what time will she be picked up, by whom, how, and when will she be taken home?

When the big night arrives, he should give special attention to his grooming. If he's paying for the whole date, he should have his money safely in hand; if they are splitting the costs, all of that should have been arranged ahead of time, so that no embarrassing moments occur.

He should be on time to pick up his date. He should not sit in the car with whoever is driving and simply honk to announce his arrival; he should go up to her house or apartment and ring the bell. Her parents will probably ask him inside, and he should sit down with them to make conversation until she arrives on the scene. If sports, for example, is the only subject about which he talks with ease, he should ask her parents what they think of such and such a team. That conversation might last well beyond the time she appears, ready to go.

During their date, he should not leave her alone or go off with other friends. He should make sure she has enough to eat and drink (unless she's the independent type who takes care of that herself). If it's a dance, he should see to it she's not standing alone on the sidelines.

He should get her home on time, exactly. If anything happens, such as transportation problems, he should assure that her parents are called immediately with an explanation of the delay.

At the end of the evening he should say, "Thank you for coming with me tonight." If the young woman doesn't thank him in return and say that *she* had a great time, then she is the one who needs to look to her manners!

I think manners are a two-way street. I think parents should be polite to us teenagers, too. My mom bursts into my room all the time when I'm talking to a friend. Isn't that bad manners, too? My friends don't even want to come to my house anymore.

I think you ought to talk this over with your mom, sometime when you're both relaxed and no one is mad at anyone. Explain that you have confidential discussions with your friends and that she should respect your right to privacy, just as I hope you respect hers. Tell her you are not doing anything in your room that you're not supposed to. (If she's worried that you are doing something illegal or harmful, like drinking and mixing it with pot, she has the right to be concerned.) Tell her you are not doing anything against the family rules, and that she should trust you. Trust brings respect—and that includes the right to one's privacy.

Our high-school daughter wears jeans, T-shirts, and docksiders to dances. I think it's terrible she doesn't ever get dressed up for anything. What can we do to make her dress properly?

As long as she is clean and decently dressed, that's all that should concern you at this point. What matters to her is that she is dressed "like all the others." Don't try to make her look different from her peers. And remember, every phase in dress fads passes and is replaced by a new one. Next year, it may be ruffles for the girls and always-a-jacket-and-tie for the boys.

What are the ingredients of a really good teen party?

Amusing invitations—creative ones that really communicate all the important information.

Good music—whether it's a stereo system, a disc jockey spinning records, or the local high-school jazz combo.

Good food—and plenty of it; plenty of good sodas and new drink ideas (no liquor), so that the absence of alcohol will not be a negative.

A good mix of guests.

Parental presence nearby (but invisible), or chaperons like some attractive college students who can be tough about any liquor or drugs smuggled into the party.

An amusing and "different" kind of theme, around which the decorations, the action, and what people wear are all organized.

One thing I've noticed is that teenagers never seem to introduce their friends to any adults. Do you think it's because they don't know how, and that makes them shy?

Yes. Young people should be trained by their parents *always* to introduce their friends who come to the house. A younger person is always presented *to* the older one: "Mom, this is my friend Anne Green. Anne, this is my mom." A student should present his parents *to* his teacher when they happen to meet. "Mr. Gallagher, this is my father, James Harding. Dad, this is Mr. Gallagher, my math teacher."

Why do so many teenagers experiment with dangerous drugs?

Peer pressure, for one thing. Boredom, for another. Then, too, young people like to "feel good," and feeling good often means that drugs are a substitute for feeling bad about something.

When young people automatically turn to something artificial to make them forget their problems and troubles, they will never learn the meaning of the word "cope." Happiness is learning how to face what is wrong, working to correct it, and then having the satisfaction of knowing one has done the best one could do.

The drug world is the antithesis of this philosophy. It can start with the harmless Saturday-night get-togethers of the group. Some people never go beyond the harmless convivial aspects of drug experimentation. Some young people go quite far beyond it—to brain damage and to death.

It is not worth "feeling good" when there are problems to face.

What is the best way to fight the drug problem?

The best place to fight drug abuse is in the family.

Parents should make themselves discuss openly and honestly the problems of drugs and alcohol when the young children are listening. Even a child in kindergarten can absorb information that might help him or her stay away from drugs later in life.

As a child matures, the parents should urge him to confide in them about any peer usage of alcohol and drugs. It takes a lot of love, support, and understanding to make a child strong enough not to partake of something "all his friends do."

It is very important for parents to notice any behavioral changes in their child as he grows older—any signals that the child may be drinking or on drugs. Any sign should be heeded immediately—with a conference at school and with any recommended counseling agencies.

Of course, along with a big dose of love, a child needs a good example at home. A child who sees Mom and Dad living it up on martinis, and fooling around with drugs at their parties needs no further drug education. It will be too late.

The Single Life

Unaccustomed solitude, for most people who have lost someone through death or rejection, can be momentarily very debilitating. Self-pity quite naturally flourishes, sapping a person's energies.

Because it is everyone's right to be happy on this earth, the newly single person should look upon this disruption in his or her life pattern as an opportunity for change, positive action, and special fulfillments.

Old hobbies and interests can be resumed; further education can open doors to new experiences. It's a time "to get one's act together," to develop an affirmative attitude. The gift of life is very precious. It should not be wasted in a long period of depression.

What are a single person's options?

The list is long. One should choose judiciously for oneself, to find the best road signs to follow to one's own goals. Among the possibilities:

1. *Get a job.* For some women, this is the most important option of all, and preparation should begin at once. It is also one of the most difficult to accomplish quickly.
2. *Increase your volunteer work.* Either move into new areas or intensify your efforts in your present field.
3. *Travel,* trying new places rather than going to familiar old places.
4. *Further your education* by taking courses you always wanted to, but never had time for. A great many museums have evening lecture series. Attending one

of these series serves as an opportunity to increase one's knowledge of the arts as well as providing an opportunity to meet new people. Courses that enhance one's chances for employment are, naturally, a priority for someone returning to the job market.

5. *Follow an intensive physical-improvement plan,* which should involve health (diet and exercise) and good looks (more exercise, new hair style and make-up, plastic surgery, and so on).

6. *Enter politics* by becoming visible in a local organization, helping candidates, and possibly laying the groundwork for running for office yourself, whether it's for the local school board or the United States Senate!

7. *Read more* and keep yourself better informed so that your conversation takes on added sparkle.

8. *Seek psychological counseling,* if you need it. Don't be ashamed to get help, but first be a good consumer and shop around for the right person, who will truly understand your needs.

9. *Become an expert at something,* whether it's Chinese export porcelain or ice skating, chess or gardening or playing the options market.

10. *Make new friends* of both sexes, which should be easy because of all the new facets of your life you are busily polishing. People will want to be around you.

11. *Rediscover your talents* in the performing and creative arts. Take up your career in singing again, go back to art classes, or reenroll in ballet school.

12. *Fix up your home environment.* If your home is badly in need of a total redecoration and you can't afford it, then redesign certain elements, which will make the interior look fresh, warm, and inviting.

13. *Entertain.* Do it well, often, and imaginatively.

14. *Buy a pet.* The right one will become your best friend and provide company at all times, as well as make living noises to break the stillness at home.

15. *Remember the house of worship of your choice.* It's the great healer of loneliness, for when you're in church, you're part of the greatest "coming together" there is.

16. *Become a volunteer.* If you are not already working

in this area, you will be helping your community, meeting new people, and making new friends. You will gain invaluable experience that will be a plus in any future career. Helping others is the greatest therapy there is for shouldering your own heavy and sad burdens.

The Widow and the Widower

When should a person who has lost a spouse begin to resume a normal life of dating and entertaining? I want to start going out again and have friends over, but I don't know how they would react to it, since my wife died only two months ago. I'm really lonely.

It wouldn't be in good taste for you to throw a large, raucous party, for example, but today everyone should feel that the widow or widower must start to lead a normal life and to entertain and go out as soon as he or she feels ready.

You are ready. Why not start off by inviting three or four close friends to dinner? Or buy some tickets to the theater or to the ballgame for two or three others—things you enjoyed doing when your wife was alive. It's your way of announcing to the world, "I'm fine. I'm standing on my own two feet again. I have a life of my own to lead—a new life—so start thinking of me in a new way."

Dating should start when you feel like it. The old traditions of a set period of mourning have gone.

What do I do about my late husband's family? They live on another coast and don't have the money to come visit us. What exactly are my responsibilities to them?

The main thing for you to do is to keep the communication lines flowing between them and your children. Keep them writing, "making presents for Grandma and Grandpa" in school. Keep snapshots going back and forth, and when your finances improve, pay for their trip to see your children, or else take your children to see them.

Even if you remarry, keep your late husband's family as part of your own.

I am a widow, about to remarry. My future husband says he feels squeamish with my late husband's photographs all over the apartment. Yet I feel it's disloyal after this many years to banish them from sight. What is the proper thing to do?

Large portraits and framed photographs of the deceased spouse should be relegated to the children's rooms (no more than one to a room). If the children are away, store those pictures to give to the children when they have their own homes.

My new husband earns much less than my late husband did, and the jewelry he can give me is very modest. Is it wrong for me to wear my late husband's engagement ring and rather handsome necklaces, earrings, and bracelets?

You should wear your present husband's jewelry. Take that big engagement ring, and when there's money enough to do it, have it reset as a pearl necklace clasp, or as a pendant for your daughter when she graduates from college, or save it for a son to give his fiancée.

When it comes to wearing your late husband's jewelry such as necklaces and bracelets to parties, it is perfectly appropriate—not, however, if your present husband has given you necklaces and bracelets, too.

Talk it over frankly with your husband. Ask him how he feels about it. Even though he may not say in words that it upsets him, you'll probably be able to tell anyway.

What does a widow call herself?

If she was born Anne Warren and married Lars Hanson, when she is widowed she is still "Mrs. Lars Hanson." However, if she remains widowed many years, she sometimes assumes the habit of calling herself "Anne Hanson," even "Mrs. Anne Hanson." A widow rarely takes back her maiden name in her social life if she used his name in married life.

On her stationery she should have her name printed as "Anne Hanson," with her address beneath. If she is writing to a commercial firm, she would sign herself "Anne Hanson," then type or print "(Mrs. Lars Hanson)" beneath her signature.

The Divorcé and Divorcée

How and when should a couple planning to divorce tell the children?

They must be told about the divorce in a calm, quiet situation, before they hear about it from someone else. They must be told that the entire family will eventually be happier with the two parents separated, that parental love will never cease, and that they, the children, will never be asked to take sides. The children should understand they'll always be taken care of.

The family social traditions should continue as long as possible with get-togethers for Christmas, Hanukkah, Easter, graduation, piano recitals, etc.

The successful human being is the one who shows intelligence, restraint, and strong affection toward his or her children, so that the shock of divorce is absorbed by those children as easily as possible.

What most upsets the divorced person's friends?

The divorced friend talking incessantly about his or her problems; demanding that friends take sides; complaining that invitations go more often to the other person than to him or her.

What about invitations and divorced couples?

Friends should try to send an equal number of invitations to each divorced spouse. If the spouse remaining in the home receives invitations in the mail from people who don't know about the divorce, it is his or her responsibility to inform the other spouse of the invitation.

It is uncomfortable for both hosts and guests if a divorced couple is invited to the same small, intimate gathering. However, a divorced couple can easily "operate" at opposite ends of the party at a *large* gathering; it is nice to invite them both.

What does a divorcée call herself?

If she was born Alice Canning and she marries and then divorces Denton Walker, she becomes "Mrs. Alice Walker," *not* "Mrs. Canning Walker." Many divorcées return to their maiden names, particularly if their former spouses and their new wives live in the same community. Often a divorced woman waits until her children are college age before returning to her maiden name, because she does not want the children's names to be different from hers—for their sake.

Some women who marry several times return to the name of a former husband a couple of marriages ago because they "like the sound of it"—because the name carries prestige. This is perfectly legal to do, but it's also a perfect way to attract criticism.

The Unmarried Live-Togethers

How should a couple be introduced when they are living together without being married?

Just as you would introduce any two separate individuals. Give each one's name, without making an editorial comment. If, however, someone asks point-blank about their relationship, such as, "Are they engaged or something?" . . . "Are those two married?" then a frank, unembroidered statement is called for: "They're living together."

Regardless of how you feel about the relationship from a moral point of view, people should be accepted and treated with kindness and consideration. It is no time to moralize and treat others differently. When families keep those precious lines of communication open with members who have chosen a life-style of which they do not approve, the element of love is the binder. Parents who "roll with the punches" manage to keep the family together. This is essential—and no matter how old a "child" may be, he or she needs that parental love as long as they live.

How do I address an invitation to two people who are living together, one invitation or two?

Address one invitation. List them alphabetically, as in this example:

> Mr. Robert Abbott
> Ms. Suzanne Elson
> 1485 Plainview
> City, state and zip

This is the order of listing which the couple should use on their mailbox and for joint bills they receive. As for telephone listings, each person should be listed in his or her own alphabetical place.

I'm living with someone and we have decided to send out joint Christmas cards. How do we have our names printed?

You'd be acting in much better taste if one of you would send out cards on behalf of the two of you. Printed names on stationery and greeting cards are for married couples, and it isn't a good idea to flout that tradition.

Is it all right, since a couple living together outside marriage are not legally bound together, to invite one person without the other?

No. A couple living together must be treated socially as an entity. It would be very rude to invite one of them to a social event without the other. A business party at lunchtime is one thing. A party on one's free time is quite another.

The Single Person Entertains and Is Entertained

Regardless of one's marital status, the ability to entertain well is a major tool of social success. The best way for a person who lives alone to receive a good number of invitations is for that person to give good parties himself or herself.

Are single men exempt from having to pay back their hosts?

Single men are no longer excused from paying back their social obligations by virtue of belonging to a desirable class—that of extra men who fill in at dinner parties to help balance the majority of single women guests. Bachelors, widowers, and divorcés should really reciprocate when their hosts entertain them repeatedly—by having them to dinner in their own homes or in restaurants or clubs.

A single person does not have to entertain everyone who has invited him or her to a party, but a repeat performance or the granting of special favors and kindnesses means one should pay back—no matter how small one's abode or how modest one's means.

Can a single person bring a date when invited to a party?

One must never bring a date to a cocktail party without calling first and asking "if it would be all right." Be prepared for the host to say, "Well, we're kind of tight for space," which is a quick signal you should heed. Don't bring a stranger to that party. They may have had to cut the list of their own friends, and it is an imposition for you to foist one of your own friends on them.

When you are invited to a lunch or dinner party, you should not bring a date, unless your host specifically says, "Is there someone you would like us to invite for you?"

Most of the time, you are being invited as a single person to fit in a special place at the party. Your hosts may have an out-of town-guest who is to be your date for the evening.

What if you're secretly engaged or living with someone, and you're invited as a single person to a party?

It is better to state immediately to your host that you are no longer to be considered in the "single category" and that you are "involved with someone, so I'm very sorry, I cannot accept your kind invitation. Thank you very much for thinking of me."

If you are straightforward with others, they will most likely ask the two of you to dinner as a couple in the near future.

What if your host asks you to bring a date and you don't know anyone to ask?

Don't be embarrassed to say that you'd "rather not bring anyone—is it all right if I just come by myself?" You might add, if you are a single woman, "You know, I really don't mind sitting next to another woman. If you don't have enough men, don't worry about it."

How does a woman pay for a man's meal in a restaurant without his getting uptight?

Once a man has been taken to lunch or dinner by a woman who acts securely about paying the bill, he tends not to be embarrassed ever again. If you sense the man you have invited is uptight about your paying for him, slip away from the table at coffee time to settle the bill with the captain, out of sight of your table. Then there won't be any hassle.

If you pay for the bill in his presence, don't spend an inordinate amount of time checking the bill (do check for errors however!), and be swift with your credit-card calculations and the tipping. The modern woman is still fighting the old—and inaccurate, for the most part—stereotype of women who do not know how to handle bill-paying and tipping.

Should I worry when the dinner table is unbalanced as to the number of men and women? There always seems to be a shortage of extra men.

Having an extra woman, or extra women, for that matter, is no sign of instant party failure. There are many more single women than men in this world, particularly when it's a question of dinner-party availability.

For a host to try to scrounge up "just any man" to round out the table is a mistake. It is far better for two women to sit next to each other at the dinner table than to ask someone at the last minute who is unattractive and who bores everyone.

Is it all right for a bachelor to entertain when he knows how to cook only a hamburger?

Absolutely. He can invite his friends and hosts to whom he is indebted without any embarrassment over his lack of culinary experience. (The same goes, of course, for a woman.) He should set an attractive table, light the candles, have everything clean and neat, and serve "the best hamburgers in town."

Great hospitality does not depend on the size of the budget; it depends on one's attitude, the quality of advance planning, a dose of imagination, and the earnest desire to please one's guests. It's far more enjoyable to be served a hamburger on a piece of inexpensive earthenware by a gracious, smiling host than to be served lobster thermidor on eighteenth-century Meissen porcelain by a grumpy, disorganized, uncaring host.

How may widows, divorcées, and single women ask men out on dates, if the men are too shy to ask them out?

It's a very simple procedure: use the telephone or the U.S. mail. If you're too embarrassed to ask a man to his face or on the telephone, write him a letter. Have something enjoyable to suggest that is your responsibility, not his, and for which he will not have to put out any money. For example:

Dear George,

My dear old aunt has given me her tickets to the symphony once again, and I was wondering if you'd like to go Tuesday, November 19. I could give you a plateful of my inimitable spaghetti beforehand, the perfect prelude to Bach and Aaron Copland.

I hope you're free. Six o'clock, my apartment.

Sincerely,
Mary

If George accepts Mary's invitation, it's up to Mary to provide all transportation and make it an expense-free evening for him.

Ceremonies of Life

The Birth of a Baby

What is the number of baby showers considered proper for a prospective mother? I have three friends, each of whom has asked me separately if she may hold a shower. Also, when are these showers supposed to be held?

One shower is enough. Why not ask your three friends (even if they don't know each other) to band together to give you *one* shower? Showers are best held in the eighth or early part of the ninth month of pregnancy, but some women are superstitious and won't allow a shower to be held in their honor until after the birth, when the baby is safely born.

I'm giving a baby shower for a friend and wonder if there are any tips on assured success. I have never even been to one before.

Like everything else in life, a successful shower requires good advance planning. Organize the presents, for one thing, so the parents won't be bombarded with fourteen rattles and sixteen bibs. Recommend useful items, not "fun things." Suggest that several friends band together to buy a major gift, like a high chair or pram that converts to a stroller. First, however, find out what the parents really need.

If your shower is held in the morning or afternoon (obviously on a Saturday or Sunday, since so many women work), serve light refreshments: iced tea or lemonade in summer; fruit juices, coffee and tea in winter, with light sandwiches and iced tea cakes.

Does the woman awaiting her second baby expect a shower?

No. She is supposed to have a lot of "necessaries" on hand from the first child, and hand-me-down clothes, too. Save your presents for the christening.

I held a baby shower for a friend at the office. Her baby lived only a few hours. Now she has come to me, asking me to help her return all the gifts. It's one of the saddest situations I've ever seen. How do we organize it and what do we say to people?

Tell her to keep all those baby things, to put them away for "the next one." That will help give the couple needed hope for the future at this tragic time in their lives.

Call or write a note on behalf of your friend to all the donors of the shower presents, and inform them of your action in persuading her to keep the baby things for the next child.

How are you supposed to announce your baby's birth, and is the sending of a birth announcement a command for a gift?

There are many ways in which a birth announcement may be made—by telephone call, Mailgram, handwritten note, "fill-in" birth-announcement card, cards that are specially printed, or formal engraved cards ordered from the stationer's. (Then, too, there are methods like that used by a friend from Chicago—the father had a sky-writer spell out the baby's name and birthdate over the Lake Michigan shoreline, from one end of the city to the other!)

The traditional engraved kind consists of a very small "calling card" with the baby's name and birthdate, which is attached by means of a satin ribbon bow (pink for a girl, blue for a boy) to a larger card with the parents' names and address. If you have twins or triplets, each one gets his or her own card and bow.

When you're ordering printed cards, you can be less traditional and can include more information, such as the birth weight, the hospital, the baby's nickname, etc. The fill-in cards from stationery departments also allow more room.

Many proud parents have copies made of the birth record

that is made in the hospital to send with the announcement.

Anyone receiving a birth announcement does *not* have to send a gift. However, a congratulatory note or telephone call is certainly in order. And if one is a close friend or relative, a gift for the baby is the nice thing to do either now or at the christening time.

What is a good godparents' present for a child?

A silver mug or silver fork-and-spoon set, engraved with the baby's initials and birthdate, is a traditional godparents' present. However, with the price of silver up in the clouds, many people have to find alternatives: an initialed porcelain mug, with the baby's birthdate under the initials, a baby book for the parents to use as a record, an album for the "first photographs of baby," a savings account opened in the baby's name (get his or her Social Security number first from the parents)—all these are good substitutes for expensive silver items.

We can't decide whether to have our baby christened in the morning or afternoon. What kind of party do we have afterward in both cases? Is the baby on display during the party?

A morning christening is usually followed by a before-lunch reception of champagne (or white wine for toasting if the budget does not permit champagne), held from eleven or eleven-thirty to one P.M. If you want to serve a small invited group lunch after the ceremony, that's nice, too.

An afternoon christening party is usually held at the cocktail hour (five to seven) with cocktails, champagne (if possible, punch if not), and hors d'oeuvres. For both morning and afternoon parties, it's nice to have a christening cake—usually white, with the baby's initials and birthdate in white icing.

The baby should be "shown off" quickly to the guests once or twice during the proceedings in his or her christening finery. It's asking too much of a small baby to keep it in the midst of a noisy, smoke-filled party for the whole period. Give the baby a break and keep it in its crib for the majority of the time.

The Young Person's Ceremonies of Life

My secretary's little girl is making her First Communion. I've been invited to the church and to lunch afterward. I'm not a Catholic, but my secretary is. Does one really have to accept a First Communion invitation? And do I bring or send a gift if I go?

You don't have to attend a First Communion ceremony—usually only the immediate family, godparents, and closest friends do. Your secretary probably asked you because she's proud to "show off" her boss to her friends, and also because she thinks (rightly or wrongly) that you would be amused and touched by the sight of the seven-year-olds looking so angelic—the girls in white veils and dresses, the boys in new suits. This is the first major religious experience of which the children themselves are aware, and it usually means a lot.

Since you were invited by your secretary to this very personal event, it would be nice to bring a present if you go, and if you don't go, to send one to the communicant. The gift needn't have religious significance—it may be anything a seven-year-old would consider nice to have, and that includes money!

I'm invited to a black-tie bar mitzvah. What's this custom all about?

A Jewish boy "comes of age" on the first Sabbath after he turns thirteen; it is one of the most important milestones of his entire life. (More girls are being "bat-mitzvahed" these days, too, at the age of thirteen, in a similar kind of ceremony.) Usually the ceremony takes place on the eve of the Sabbath; then, after the Sabbath worship service, the child (and immediate family) receive congratulations from members of the congregation. This is often followed by a luncheon or dinner to which close friends and relatives are invited.

Since yours is a black-tie affair, it means that everyone at dinner will be in formal dinner clothes. You should bring a gift or send it (far easier for the recipient and his family). A check is also gratefully received.

The Debutante

I'm a college student and have been invited to be the number-one escort for a girl who is "making her debut," whatever that means, at a big dance this Christmas with some other girls. I wish I knew what my obligations as "number-one escort" are.

In former days, a young woman made her debut at approximately the age of eighteen as a signal to the world she was ready for a husband. Today, it does not mean that at all, but rather that a young woman of good social standing (with a parent who has enough money) wants to have a year of great fun and constant partying. Today's young college women for the most part have careers rather than immediate marriage on their minds.

You should send flowers to the debutante's home on the day of her party (or the day after), with your card and a personal message. (It can be as short as "I am honored to be taking the prettiest girl in town to her debut.")

As her number-one escort, you may well have to rent white tie and tails; she will brief you well ahead on when you have to show up for a rehearsal of the pageant or presentation program for the ball.

You and her other escorts (there may be two or three more) should see to it that she is danced off her feet, never left alone, and that she will have memories of her debut night as the greatest fun of her life.

"You should oversee the transportation of your group from wherever you were invited to dinner beforehand to the place where the ball is being held. Afterward, you should invite the debutante and her best friend and escorts to "breakfast" or some more late-night dancing. (The deb's father will often slip you the money for this; if not, be prepared to pay for it yourself; it should be your only expense for the evening.)

I am invited to my niece's debut party. Does this call for a present from her uncle and me?

Since you are really close relatives, it is nice to send her a personal gift. A piece of jewelry is the best, but since that is too expensive for many people, a bottle of perfume, some pretty bottles for her bathroom, a pair of white gloves (for Christmas parties), a sweater—anything that she will feel is a "pampering gift"—is suitable.

No one except close relatives and godparents is expected to give presents to the debutante.

Aren't debutante teas a thing of the past?

No, they are still being held, especially in certain places in the South. At these parties, usually held at home, the debutante's mother and female relatives receive at a candlelit tea. The debutante and her friends dress in long formal dresses; she usually carries a bouquet. It sounds old-fashioned, but it is gracious and pretty.

What does a girl do who doesn't want to spend a great deal of money on a fancy coming-out ball?

She usually finds out what the total bill would be for the party, her dress, and all the other extras (posed formal portrait, bouquet, etc.), and then tells her parents she'll take half the money and "instead go to Europe next summer."

The Engagement

Who hosts the official engagement party? When should it be held? What kind of party should it be?

Usually the parents of the bride-to-be or a close relative gives the party. The best date for an engagement party is the day before it is being announced in the newspaper. Since most papers announce engagements on Sunday, that means Saturday.

It's most often a simple cocktail party. If the hosts can afford champagne, it's nice to bring it out at one point during the party, give each guest a glass, and make toasts to the pair for a happy future.

What kind of invitation is appropriate for an engagement party?

You may do handwritten invitations on your notepaper, or you may use the fill-in invitations from the stationer's. If the announcement is to be a surprise, mention nothing about the engagement. If the groom-to-be is from out of town, for example, you could write "to meet Mr. John Lewis" in the upper-left-hand corner of the invitation, without divulging the secret.

If you want everyone to know it's an engagement party, write on your invitation "in honor of Mary Jones and John Lewis" just beneath the line that reads you are inviting people "to cocktails" or "to a reception."

We are giving an engagement party for my goddaughter, whose parents are dead. What can we do to make it an extra-special event and not just an ordinary cocktail party?

You might have some favors made that utilize the couple's joint initials (like book matches or plastic champagne glasses). If you can obtain a baby picture of each without their knowing it, you can have each one blown up to poster size and use the pair of them as the best kind of wall decorations. T-shirts transfer-printed with snapshots of the pair as they are today are also a popular "giveaway."

When does a woman wear her ring in public for the first time?

The "unveiling" of the engagement ring traditionally occurs at the engagement party. (Lots of oohs and aahs as background music!)

My fiancé can't afford an engagement ring right now. He says we shouldn't announce our engagement until he can buy me one. He says if I don't have one, it will make him look like a financial failure. What is your opinion?

Tell your fiancé that millions and millions of young women (including myself, who was not so young) married without ever owning an engagement ring. Tell your friends you intend to have a jeweled wedding band instead of an engagement ring, and if there are no stones in the wedding band, it doesn't matter. After eighteen years of marriage with only a gold wedding ring on my left hand, I can tell you it does not matter.

How do you send an engagement announcement to the papers?

The newspapers in each city have their own formats, deadlines, and policy about announcing engagements. Call the women's-page editor and ask how far ahead they need copy and exactly what they want. Some papers send you a form to fill out.

Be sure to type your announcement with home address and business-telephone number. Follow the format of your newspaper, which generally consists of the following information: the names of the affianced pair; your home towns; date of the wedding (either specific or in general terms like "next winter," or perhaps the phrase "No date has been set for the wedding"); the names of both of your schools; your parents' professions; your own occupations or company affiliations.

Many large papers in major metropolitan centers like New York, Los Angeles, and Chicago announce very few engagements, so couples should steel themselves for disappointment in this respect. Some newspapers make you pay for the announcement.

How is an engagement announced in the paper when one's parents are divorced and remarried, or a parent is deceased?

In the case of divorced parents: "Mrs. John d'Onofrio announces the engagement of her daughter Pamela Caswell to George Smith. Miss Caswell is also the daughter of Mr. Timothy Caswell of Philadelphia . . ."

In the case of a deceased father and a remarried mother: "Mrs. Steven Jacobs announces the engagement of her daughter Jennifer Miller to Alfred Schmidt. Miss Miller is also the daughter of the late Mr. Jonathan Miller. . . ."

In the case of the groom-to-be's parents being divorced: ". . . to David Brock, son of Mrs. Joan Brock of this city and Mr. Gustave Brock of New Orleans . . ."

In the case of one of the fiancé's parents being deceased: ". . . to Stanfield Johnson, son of Mr. Danton Johnson and the late Mrs. Johnson. . . ."

When you're marrying the second time, may you send in an engagement announcement to the papers, and may you have an engagement party?

Newspapers carry a second-time-around engagement announcement only if one or both are very prominent in the city and therefore are a news item, not just a social item. As for an "engagement party" the second time around, it is much nicer to call it simply a "party" that is a prewedding celebration.

Engagement celebrations per se are really for the first-time-around brides. If the bride-to-be's fiancé has been divorced, but she has not been married previously, it is appropriate for the couple to announce a formal engagement at a party in their honor.

If an engagement is broken, does the ring have to be returned?

Yes, it really should be. Any expensive jewelry given by one to the other in connection with a marriage commitment should be returned.

How does one tell the world that an engagement is broken? I've seen it placed in a newspaper ad, and I've received printed announcements, too.

The old-fashioned ways are the best: have your friends pass the word around. To your really close friends and family out of town, write a short note. You don't have to say much or tell reasons why. Something like this will do: "Jane and I have decided it's better not to go ahead with our marriage plans. We know it's for the best." . . . "Larry and I found it just wasn't working out the way it should. We reached a mutual decision to call it off, but we're still great friends."

No blame should be affixed to the other person, and no criticisms should be leveled. It's a time to act in a considerate and controlled manner.

_____

INVITATIONS

If the wedding is going to be small and modest, what kind of invitation do you use?

A personal note on good-quality notepaper (white or cream-colored) is perfectly proper to use as an invitation. The bride might write notes to the younger generation, and her mother might write the notes for her generation. The message might be something as simple as this note from the bride's mother to the bride's aunt:

> Mary and Jack will be married in a small informal ceremony Saturday, August 14, at four o'clock at St. Thomas'. All of us, of course, want you, Bill, and the children there to share the happy occasion with us.
>
> Afterward we'll drink a toast to the bride and groom at our house. I have enclosed a plane and a bus schedule, and we'll get you put up for the night with friends.
>
> As you undoubtedly know, Mary feels she can't get married without you there!
>
> Love,
> Carol

If the wedding is last-minute in its organization, the bride's parents may send the invitation to the group in a Mailgram, or if time is *really* short, the invitation should be extended on the telephone!

When should invitations be put in the mail?

Invitations to a large wedding—particularly in a big city where peoples' schedules become filled far in advance—should be mailed six to eight weeks in advance. This allows close friends and family who live in other cities the time to make their plans to travel to the wedding site. It allows business people the opportunity to "hold the date" in their busy calendars.

What determines whether you send engraved or printed invitations?

The budget and the amount of time you have available. If you can afford engraved invitations ordered from the stationer's, and if you order them far enough in advance (ten to twelve weeks prior to the wedding date), engraved invitations are the best. This is one time in your life when "it's great to go first class."

How do you compile a wedding list? We don't know where to start. Between the groom's side of the family and our side, the bride's, we must have a list of a thousand friends. Yet we can't afford a reception for more than two hundred people.

The wedding list is the bride's responsibility, as far as compilation is concerned. Half the invitations go to the groom's side, of course. If you know your budget will allow for two hundred people, then order enough invitations for 225 people (your acceptances will average about two hundred). You should also order invitations for those people who should receive one even though you know they can't make the wedding (good friends who live far away, elderly people who are not mobile, etc.).

Be sure the final list that goes to whoever is addressing the envelopes by hand is neatly typed, alphabetized, with a full address and zip code for every name. Don't forget to check the list for accuracy in titles, too, such as "Dr." and "The Hon.," etc., whenever it is appropriate.

How do you decide who gets an invitation and who gets an announcement?

The "musts" get invitations—members of the wedding party, of course, family, godparents, the couple's college roommates, perhaps a member of management and close associates in the couple's places of business, their intimate social friends, and the parents' closest friends.

Keep cutting back that list until you reach the desired number, and put the other names on the "Announcement Recipients" list. Tell everyone from the beginning that your wedding will be "a very small one," so that those who aren't invited aren't offended.

Is it all right to bring a date to a wedding?

No, if your date is unknown to the bride or groom, it would be extremely rude. The wedding lists are edited with a fine-tooth comb, and the bride and groom's families can't even ask all their friends. Therefore, they would hardly welcome one of their guests bringing along an uninvited guest!

How is the decision made as to who gets invited to the church and the reception and who gets invited to the church only?

In many weddings, the guests are invited to the church and then greet the bride and groom and toast them with punch in the back parlors of the church. The custom of inviting guests to the church only and then inviting a certain few to a reception in a club or hotel is disappearing, because those who get all dressed up for the church service and then watch certain ones go on to a reception may become offended.

Often, however, when it's a second marriage, the couple has a small religious service attended only by the family and three or four close friends, and then a large reception is held, to which all the couple's friends are invited.

If my husband and I receive a wedding invitation, are our children automatically included?

No. If their names aren't on the outside envelope of an informal invitation, or on the inside envelope of a formal invitation, they are not invited, and your bringing them would be a mistake. If your whole family is invited, your and your husband's names only would be on the outer stamped envelope, such as: Mr. and Mrs. Frank A. Smith. The inner envelope, however, would bear the names of any children under the age of eighteen who are to be invited, along with the parents' names (note that on the inner envelope, the first name of the parents is omitted):

> Mr. and Mrs. Smith
> James and Mary

Children who are eighteen and over would receive their own invitations. If they live at the same address, one invitation will suffice. On the outer envelope they would be addressed as follows:

Mr. James Smith and Miss Mary Smith
Address

On the inner envelope one would write:

Mr. Smith and Miss Smith

The inner envelope for two brothers at the same address would read:

The Messrs. Smith

The inner envelope for two sisters at the same address would read:

The Misses Smith

One may always use "Ms." as a substitute for "Miss." Since there is no plural for "Ms.," one would have to repeat the given names of the women on the inside envelope:

Ms. Anne Smith and Ms. Mary Smith

How should the envelopes of wedding invitations and announcements look? Isn't it all right if my secretary types the addresses?

No, the envelopes should really be addressed by hand (and by someone with a beautiful handwriting) in black ink. The envelopes should be hand-stamped. For this occasion, a typed address and metered postage are too cold and businesslike.

Remember that in addressing an envelope for a wedding invitation or an announcement, abbreviations are not used (except for Mr., Mrs., Dr., Jr., or Lt. when combined with Colonel). Words like "Street," "Avenue," and the names of states are written out, too.

Be sure to put the return address on the front of the envelope, in the upper-left-hand corner, *not* on the back flap. This is to help the post office return misaddressed envelopes more efficiently.

Would you please give me an example of a wedding-and-reception-invitation text?

Your invitation might look like this:

> Mr. and Mrs. Henry Frank Upton
> request the honour of your presence
> at the marriage of their daughter
> Jessica
> to
> Mr. David John O'Hara
> on Saturday, the fifth of June
> at four o'clock
> Saint James's Church
> San Francisco
> and afterward at
> The Fairmont Hotel

RSVP
1000 Mason Street
San Francisco, California zip code

I am divorced and remarried. My husband and I will be giving the wedding, but my former husband, the bride's father, and his new wife will be giving the reception. How do we word such a complicated invitation?

You would start off with the wedding invitation done in this manner:

> Mr. and Mrs. Norman Hans Greene
> request the honour of your presence
> at the marriage of Mrs. Greene's daughter
> Amantha Grace Kenyon
> to
> Et cetera (and don't forget to
> have the RSVPs go to the Greenes)

Then you would enclose a separate reception card that would read:

> Mr. and Mrs. Henry Cabot Kenyon
> request the pleasure of your company
> immediately following the ceremony
> at Fifteen Greenwood Avenue
> Bronxville

RSVP

Acceptances and regrets for both events would be sent to one place: the bride's mother. She would naturally inform the bride's father and his wife of the acceptances and regrets for the reception.

We want to invite a large group to the church ceremony for our daughter and future son-in-law, followed by a brief reception in the back parlors of the church. We also want to invite some fifty people to a wedding lunch afterward in our club. How do we handle the invitations?

Invitations would read something like the following for *all* guests:

Mr. and Mrs. Anthony Lockwood Green
request the honour of your presence
at the marriage of their daughter
Monica Anne
to
Mr. Raymond Philip Danton
on Saturday, the eighth of October
at twelve o'clock
Saint John's Church
on Hillwood Lane
and afterward in the parlors of the church

RSVP
4261 Ninth Avenue
Des Moines, Iowa zip code

Those who are being invited to the lunch would receive an additional, smaller card enclosed in their invitation which might read as follows:

Mr. and Mrs. Anthony Lockwood Green
request the pleasure of your company
at the wedding luncheon
following the church-parlor reception
at
The Links Country Club

RSVP

How do we communicate the fact that our daughter's wedding reception will be a dinner?

When a four-o'clock wedding is followed by a wedding reception that includes dinner, it is advisable to say so on the invitations. Otherwise guests may leave, with their own dinner plans. State on the invitation or on the separate reception card: "Reception and dinner immediately following the ceremony."

I am being married in Rome. We will be back in my hometown briefly two weeks later, and my parents want to give me a wedding reception then. What kind of invitations do they send?

"Late receptions" or "second receptions" are usually informal cocktail parties. You would be the honored guests. Your parents would put "For Mr. and Mrs. John Cutler Anderson" in the upper-left corner of their invitation "to a reception."

If their party will be a small one, telephoned invitations are perfectly proper, too.

The groom's parents are paying for half the wedding expenses, and they feel their names should be included somehow on the invitation. Also, my name, the bride's mother's, is different from my daughter's, since I've remarried. The groom's mother is also remarried. How should the invitation read?

You might do it as follows:

Mr. Malcolm Connell Baldwin and
Mrs. James Lee Anderson
request the honour of your presence
at the marriage of their daughter
Mary Frances
to
Mr. James Bouvier King
son of
Mr. Francois Didier King and Mrs. Gordon Lyn Smith
on Saturday, the seventh of May
et cetera

A divorced friend of mine recently married a single woman. They were married in a large church wedding; she wore a long white dress and veil. Now I am being remarried myself and I want to send out engraved wedding invitations, since my first wedding was small and informal (as well as disastrous). Is this all right to do?

I'm afraid it's more appropriate for you *not* to send those engraved wedding invitations. Tradition decrees that only a first-time bride may have all the trappings of a formal wedding ceremony; a woman who has been married before should be married more quietly. A man who has married before may participate in a second (and even third) formal wedding, if his bride is being married for the first time.

Your parents may issue engraved *reception* invitations for your second wedding. The text might read something like this:

> Mr. and Mrs. Angus McKenzie
> request the pleasure of your company
> at a reception
> following the marriage of their daughter
> Maria McKenzie Sims
> to
> Mr. Robert Morris Fenwick
> on Friday, the tenth of December
> et cetera

I am a widow, marrying a widower. May we send out our own wedding invitations to our very large families?

Yes. The wording might be something like this:

> Mrs. George Andrew Kiser
> and
> Mr. Franklin Drew Ryan
> request the pleasure of your company
> at a reception following their marriage

If you wish to have them present at the ceremony as well, you might word the invitations like this:

> The honour of your presence
> is requested at the marriage of
> Mrs. George Andrew Kiser
> to
> Mr. Franklin Drew Ryan
> on Saturday, the first of April
> at four o'clock
> Church of Saint John's
> and afterward at
> The Maidstone Club
> Easthampton

RSVP
Fourteen Peacock Lane
Easthampton, New York zip code

You may send out announcements of your wedding to your friends using the same form, *i.e.*, "Mrs. George Andrew Kiser and Mr. Franklin Drew Ryan announce their marriage, Saturday, April first," etc.

My daughter is a medical doctor. Should her title be included on her formal wedding invitations?

Yes, her title, "Doctor" or "Dr.," would precede her name.
A woman who is a Ph.D. may also use "Doctor" in front of her name, but many people find that pretentious, so not too many do it.

I'm a widower. How do I have my daughter's wedding invitations worded? She also wants her Air Force rank included on the invitations.

The following might be an appropriate way:

> Mr. Grant Burton Malmgren
> requests the honour of your presence
> at the marriage of his daughter
> Jennifer
> Lieutenant, United States Air Force
> on Thursday, the fourth of October
> et cetera

What are the rules governing the way in which a military person's title and branch of service are put on formal invitations, such as for weddings?

A junior officer's rank is placed on a line beneath his name:

Henry Miller Bernstein
Lieutenant, United States Army

A person with a rank higher than lieutenant has the title listed before his or her name:

Capt. (or Captain) Mary Anne Bigelow
United States Navy

It's optional whether you list the branch of service or not on wedding invitations. For example, you can either put "United States Army" or "Artillery, United States Army," beneath the officer's name and title.

Does a "noncom" have to put his or her grade and service-branch information on a wedding invitation?

You can put just your name and branch of service beneath it, for example:

Stephen Clay Bowers
United States Marine Corps

or you might prefer to put:

Stephen Clay Bowers
Staff Sergeant, United States Marine Corps

Women officers and noncommissioned officers follow the same rules for their listings as for the men.

What are "At Home" cards, anyway?

They are small cards sometimes included in wedding announcements, sometimes included in wedding invitations, too, particularly if the couple will be living abroad, or even in another city.

At Home cards are very useful. They communicate the pair's new place of residence; they tell recipients the date they will be in residence (and not on a honeymoon). If the new telephone number is known, it should be included.

The cards provide the proper address for the sending of wedding presents for those who did not send them before the wedding.

If a woman decides to keep her maiden name, the At Home card communicates this fact very deftly. For example:

> Mr. Kurt Brown and Miss Penelope Ribes
> after the first of May
> Fourteen Washington Square
> New York, New York zip
> Telephone: (212) 000-0000

We live quite far out in the country, and we wondered if it were proper form to include a map in a formal wedding invitation?

Yes, it's a great idea, both to show guests how to find the church and the place of the reception. For a formal wedding invitation, the map should be printed on good stock (the same as the invitation itself). For an informal wedding invitation, it may be duplicated on any kind of machine and tucked into the invitation.

What if you're giving an outdoor wedding but have alternate plans in case of rain?

Have a separate little card printed, and insert it inside the invitation. It might read as follows:

> In case of rain
> the wedding will be held
> in
> St. Mary's-of-the-Sea Church
> and the reception will be held
> at
> 1462 Highwood Avenue
> the residence of Mr. and Mrs. John Smith
> Please check at this number: (000) 000-0000

Help! Our daughter is having second thoughts about her forth-coming marriage. The invitations were sent out a few weeks ago. If worse comes to worst, how do we call it off as grace-fully as possible?

You have a big job ahead of you if the wedding is but a few days off. Ask some friends to help you, split your wedding lists into sections, and have them call everyone on the list. If you have six weeks to spare, you may send out a printed or engraved card that reads:

Dr. and Mrs. Stephen Landon Thorne
announce that the marriage of their daughter
Stephanie
to
Mr. George Baker Tubbs
by mutual consent
will not take place

If you have a week to spare, you could send everyone on your invitation list a Mailgram, using the same message as the one given above.

What about postponements?

Again, if a wedding has to be postponed because of a death, sickness, or a required absence from the city, the same system of notifying people—by telephone, by announcement card, or by Mailgram—would be used.

Our friends are very bad about RSVP-ing to invitations. Is it acceptable to include in each of our daughter's invitations a fill-in acceptance or regret card, plus a stamped, self-addressed envelope?

The fill-in acceptance card may be fine for business func-tions, and I know it is being used more and more with wedding invitations, but it's a very sad trend.

Many people feel that this is a lazy, even slovenly way of handling one's social obligations. Do as you wish in this situa-tion, but I would hope that your friends would think enough of you and your daughter to sit down, to put pen to paper, and to spend five minutes telling you whether or not they can come to the wedding!

WEDDING ANNOUNCEMENTS

How do we word formal wedding announcements for our daughter and future son-in-law? They will be married quietly because of a death in our family, but we want to send out several hundred announcements. Also, is it necessary to send separate announcements to all the people in their respective offices who are close to them? That would require a lot of announcements!

Following is the text of a traditional formal wedding announcement. Remember, these must not be mailed until immediately *after* the wedding ceremony, never before:

Mr. and Mrs. Farwell Dean Blubreck
have the honour of announcing
the marriage of their daughter
Ann Marie
to
Mr. Richard Carter Mooney
on Saturday, the twelfth of March
One thousand nine hundred eighty-one
Saint John's Church (optional)
Akron

If your daughter and son-in-law wish to communicate their new address and telephone number, that may also be done by enclosing a small "At Home" card with the announcement.

As for imparting the news to their office friends, one should be sent to the personnel office or to an executive friend at each place, with a request that it be posted on an employee bulletin board or in some central spot for all to see.

We eloped and are estranged from our parents on both sides. We are both successful in our careers and feel like sending out formal engraved announcements of our marriage, in spite

*of our parents. Is this done? I might also add that I am re-
taining my maiden name.*

Your formal announcements might be worded in this manner:

Miss (or Ms.) Mary Jane Howell
and
Dr. James Edward O'Meara
announce their marriage
on Thursday, the fourth of August
One thousand nine hundred and eighty-one
Chicago (you may mention the name of
the church if you wish to)

One way to communicate the retention of your maiden name
is to enclose an At Home card that might read as follows:

Ms. Mary Jane Howell
Dr. James Edward O'Meara
At Home
after the twentieth of August
4435 Simonton
Dallas, Texas zip
Telephone number: (optional)

*We are middle-aged widowed people who are getting married.
We want to send out announcements of our happy news. My
parents announced my first marriage. Happily, both are still
alive. Do they announce this marriage, too?*

No, you would announce your own marriage, in the same
fashion as Mary Jane Howell and Dr. James Edward O'Meara
(see previous example).

*I'm a widow. My daughter, also widowed, is marrying again,
I'm happy to say. How should her wedding announcements be
worded?*

You would include your daughter's full name, not just her
given name, on the announcements.

Mrs. Jonathon Schwartz
has the honour of announcing
the marriage of her daughter
Ann Schwartz Miller
to
Jeremy Sedgwick Reece
on Wednesday, the second of May
Tulsa, Oklahoma

When are you supposed to mail announcements?

Have a family friend put them in a mailbox immediately *after* the wedding has taken place. It's a nice touch if the envelope bears the same postmark date as the wedding.

Since weddings on rare occasions are canceled at the last minute, it's tempting fate to mail the announcements before the wedding actually takes place.

Engraved or printed announcements can be mailed out up to four months after the wedding. After that date, it's better for the married couple to inform any friends they forgot by a personal note.

WEDDING ACCEPTANCES AND REGRETS

We received our first invitation to a very formal wedding and reception, and we don't know how to reply. It's long and complicated, isn't it?

No, it's short and easy. Let's take a hypothetical formal wedding invitation and a hypothetical formal acceptance and regret.

Doctor and Mrs. Grant Andrew Lewis
request the honour of your presence
at the marriage of their daughter
Diana
to
Mr. John Ames Williams
on Saturday, the tenth of May
One thousand nine hundred and eighty-one
at four o'clock
Saint Thomas More
New York

and afterward at
The Colony Club
62nd and Park Avenue

RSVP
450 Park Avenue
New York City 10022

Acceptances and regrets to formal invitations should be hand-written on good notepaper, in black or dark blue ink. The message should be centered. The envelope is addressed to the parents of the bride or to whoever's name is at the top of the invitation.

If you are accepting the wedding invitation, your acceptance would look like this:

Mr. & Mrs. Robert Baldwin
accept with pleasure
Doctor and Mrs. Grant Andrew Lewis'
kind invitation for
Saturday, the tenth of May

If you are regretting the wedding, your note could read as follows:

Mr. & Mrs. Robert Baldwin
regret that they are unable to accept
Doctor and Mrs. Grant Andrew Lewis'
kind invitation for
Saturday, the tenth of May

You may write in an excuse for not being able to accept, such as:

sincerely regret that
their absence from the city
prevents their accepting
Doctor and Mrs. Grant Andrew Lewis'
kind invitation for
et cetera

or:

sincerely regret that
illness in the family
prevents their accepting
et cetera

The formal acceptance or regret notes are very important, in that the job of keeping the tally of guests for a large wedding usually falls to someone's secretary or retained adviser. These notes are the most efficient way for an outside person to keep accurate records. However, a personal letter to the parents of the bride or to the bride or the groom explaining how sorry you are not to be able to be there is the nice way to do it— along *with* the formal note of regret.

We received a Mailgram invitation to a friend's daughter's wedding. The wedding was planned so quickly, they didn't have time to have invitations made and mailed. Do I send a formal acceptance to that kind of invitation?

No, in this case you'd send a warm note saying that of course you and your husband will be there, that you wouldn't miss it for the world; you would state how pleased you are to be able to share in an exciting and happy event.

If you receive an informal note or a Mailgram or a telephone call inviting you to a wedding, even if you say yes on the telephone, you should write that informal note saying "yes" to go on the record as having accepted.

If you're sending a formal acceptance to someone's wedding to which your children have been invited too, and only some of the children are able to attend, how do you communicate this in the reply?

You might send a formal reply worded like this:

Mr. and Mrs. Robert Miller
Anita and Robert, Jr.
accept with pleasure
the kind invitation
of Mr. and Mrs. Carmine Fabrizio
for
Saturday, the twentieth of November
at twelve o'clock
Jennifer and William
regret that they are unable to attend

WEDDING PLANS: WHO PAYS

The parents of the girl I'm going to marry cannot afford the kind of wedding she and I want very much to have. My own parents have offered to give us the wedding. I would like to know if the groom's family can pay for the wedding? If so, does my mother run it?

Tradition has always decreed that the bride's family pays for most of the wedding costs; however, common sense prevails today, and whoever can pay either pays a major share of the expenses or all of the expenses. The matter must be handled tactfully with the bride's parents. Ask your parents to speak to them right now, in an open and frank discussion, before the wedding plans have been finalized. They should state exactly what they are in a position to pay—perhaps all the expenses.

However, everyone must realize that the wedding plans must still be made primarily by the bride and her mother, not by the groom's side of the family. Keep your conversations within the confines of the two families, too. It's a private matter, not for friends to know about.

I divorced my wife many years ago, and have remarried. Now that my daughter from the first marriage is getting married, her mother is hounding me to pay for the entire wedding. Exactly what are my obligations in this matter?

It's up to you—to your financial status, to your relationship with your daughter, and to any number of things. It depends on whether you have been paying alimony for a good number of years; it depends on the financial situation of your ex-wife, as well as your own.

Sometimes a father in a case like this pays for the reception or the honeymoon. Talk the matter over with your ex-wife—right now. It's a time for compromise—for her sake.

WEDDING PLANS: THE CHURCH

Who decides on where the wedding will be held?

The bride usually chooses her own church and her clergyman to marry her and her fiancé, unless the groom is a clergyman himself or the son of one, in which case the wedding would be held in his church.

Both the bride and groom should visit the clergyman together to decide on the ceremony, special prayers, music, etc.

If the wedding is to be held in a public place like a hotel, a hall, or a restaurant, the couple should be elastic about the date and the hour of the wedding, because of the possibility of previous bookings.

What determines the hour of the wedding?

In the South and West, evening weddings held in a church or at home are popular. In the East, many fashionable Protestant weddings take place at four, four-thirty, or five in the afternoon. Jews do not marry on their Sabbath (Friday sundown through Saturday sundown), nor on their high holy days. Catholic weddings (particularly if a nuptial mass is involved) are usually held in the mornings, up through noon, followed by breakfast or lunch; lavish Christian weddings are usually not held during Lent.

How extensive do the church floral decorations have to be, and who pays for them?

When decorating of the altar is permitted, putting some flowers on and around it may be all the flowers needed. Sometimes the florist will decorate the front reserved pews with greenery and flowers. (If you're watching your budget, go heavy on the greenery and easy on the blossoms.)

The bride's family traditionally pays for the church decoration, but if there is another wedding or two in the church the same day as yours, arrange to have the mothers of the brides meet, plan on a mutual decor with one designer involved, and split the costs equally among you and the other brides.

For my own wedding, we didn't have to buy flowers for the church. We were married on December 27, and the entire church was ablaze with crimson poinsettia plants banked everywhere. There was even a ten-foot-tall pyramid of them on the main altar, thanks to the Christmas season!

I've seen canopies stretching from the church door to the street curb. Is that a "must" at large weddings? And is the canvas carpet down the main aisle of the church necessary?

Both are nice touches for large formal weddings, but neither is a necessity.

The florist will supply the canvas runner, but the ushers lay it as soon as the bride's mother has been seated and the wedding procession is to start. The runner is, of course, to save the bride's train from being soiled. It is symbolic more than anything else. It is laid slightly on one side of the main aisle—the side the bride uses to walk down on her father's arm.

May I select my own music for the wedding?

In many churches, only rigidly prescribed music may be played by the church organist. In other churches, there are rules prohibiting the singing of solos. The organist should be consulted, because he or she will know the rules and will know what is appropriate. A fee must be paid to the organist, as well as to any soloists or choir that may have been selected.

Who pays for the church use and for the clergyman who officiates?

The bride's family pays for the use of the church (sexton's fee); the decor; the music; and anything rented, such as the canopy and carpeting; gratuities to the policemen directing traffic outside the church; and limousine service for the bridal party to and from the church.

The groom is traditionally supposed to pay for the clergyman's fee and tips to the altar boys. Often the groom is in such a nervous state, the bride's family takes over this responsibility, too.

WEDDING PRESENTS

I have two questions to ask about an invitation I received to the church service only. First, do I have to send an RSVP, and second, do I have to send a present if I go to the church?

The answer to both questions is no.

Do you have to send a present if you're invited to a wedding and reception but you can't be there?

Officially, no. However, the giving of a wedding gift should be predicated upon friendship and good wishes rather than on value given for value received.

I have a lot of friends who are being married for the second time now, some for the third. I certainly don't have to keep sending wedding presents, do I, even if they invite me to their receptions?

No, but here again, it's a question of friendship. If you send a small token, with a note of good wishes for their happiness, you are going on record as accepting their new union and supporting their actions. This means a great deal to people who have remarried. They are often worried about "how their friends feel about it." Marriage is a time to support one's friends, to wish them well, and to hope it's "for keeps." Spend a very small amount of money, but put some thought into your note that goes with the gift. You won't regret it, and they'll love you for it.

We would like to have a formal showing of our daughter's wedding presents when they arrive. She will receive many lovely presents and many sizable checks. We want our friends to know how generous everyone has been. Is this appropriate today? Not too many people seem to do it.

It is still "correct" to do it. Cover a large table (in a room in your house devoted to the presents) with a shiny white fabric (a silk or satiny cloth). It looks pretty to decorate the table-cloth edge with an occasional white bow or cluster of orange blossoms.

Display the presents with the cards of the donors attached. Checks should not be displayed. You might have a typed list of the names of the people who sent checks. Do not put in the amounts.

One reason presents aren't displayed as much as they used to be is that some people feel it is a little materialistic. An even greater restraint is that word gets around too fast to the criminal element in town. There have been some grandstand robberies of houses with wedding-present displays!

Should our daughter list her choices in the bridal registries of the stores? Isn't that materialistic?

No, it helps make everything more efficient. It helps the purchaser feel secure about the present—that it's something the bride and groom really wanted. It also avoids duplication (the nine-water-pitchers syndrome). It also helps the bride purchase her sterling flatware, which is terribly expensive. Most brides would prefer to have two or three friends go in together on purchasing one knife in the bride's desired pattern than to go off into the blue to find something that may be only a dust-catcher in the couple's lives.

It's less confusing if the bride registers at just one store in town (or in one store selling each type of merchandise, *i.e.*, sterling, china and crystal, or gourmet kitchenware).

What if the bride has not registered and you don't have a clue as to what to get a couple for their wedding?

Ask the bride or the groom, without any sense of embarrassment. Say something like, "What do you really need? More crystal? What kind? A contribution toward your sterling flatware? Bedding, or what?" You might end up being the donor of something they really want—like the radio for their new car, or an electric blanket.

If you can't afford what the bride or groom suggests, then go in with another friend or relative on the present.

Is it all right to trust one's own taste in selecting art for the home of the engaged couple?

It's better not to. If you want to furnish them with something nice for their walls, give them a gift certificate to the art store and let them pick it out themselves.

When should you send a wedding gift?

The best time to send it is immediately after receiving the invitation. Then you won't forget. If you are going to select something from a store with a bridal registry where the bride-to-be has already made her selections, you know you won't be making a mistake.

*I don't have much money, and I'd like to send my best friend's
daughter something from among my own treasured possessions. Will she think that I'm being cheap and that I'm giving
her some old "secondhand" object?*

Any young woman of taste and good breeding appreciates
a well-made object from the past. Your friend's daughter
would probably consider it a great honor to receive one of
your "treasured possessions." Tell her in an accompanying
note that this object has always been one of your favorite
things. Chances are, it will become one of *her* favorite things.

*Is it all right to bring one's wedding present to the reception,
if one has been tardy in purchasing it?*

No, it's far better to send your present to the bride's parents'
home or to the newlyweds' home. If you bring your present
to the reception, one of the bridal party has to keep track of it,
and the chances are too high of your card being separated from
the present, and of your present being broken, misplaced, or
stolen.

*What's the deadline on thank-you notes for wedding presents,
and what about the sending of those formal gift-acknowledg-
ment cards?*

The thank-you note for a wedding gift should be written
within two or three weeks, if possible. (The smart bride keeps
up with her notes until the actual wedding date.)

Three months is about the outside time within which one
should expect an acknowledgment. I am all for husbands
splitting the task of writing the thank-you notes, if the wives
work.

The acknowledgment card (usually engraved) is for great
big weddings, with hundreds of presents involved. If it's sent
out after the wedding, the bride and groom's married names
are used:

> Mr. and Mrs. Johnson Fitzhugh Coleman
> wish to acknowledge the receipt
> of your lovely wedding gift
> and will write a personal note of thanks
> at an early date

If you are one of the above, don't forget, of course, to send that personal handwritten note within the three-month grace period.

Do you have some ideas for presents we can give our ushers and bridesmaids? Do the maid of honor, the matron of honor, and the best man receive something special, unlike the gifts for the rest of the wedding-party?

Your special attendants should receive something a little different, a little better, than the rest of the party. For example, if you're giving your bridesmaids little silver pocket mirrors, you might give your maid and matron of honor small silver compacts. If the groom is giving his ushers silver keychains, he might give his best man a small silver stud box.

Anything small in silver (or *very* small in gold) that may be engraved with the couple's initials and the date of the wedding is a great item to give bridal attendants—for example, keyrings, bangle bracelets, earring boxes, pin trays, or letter openers for the young women, and tie clips, bar knives, jiggers, belt buckles, for the young men. Gifts of glass etched with the wedding date and the wedding pair's initials are also wonderful presents, ones which will always evoke memories of that particular day.

What are the bride and groom supposed to give each other for their wedding, and when do they exchange these gifts?

If the bride and groom are up to their ears in wedding bills, they don't give each other a present. If they are financially able to buy a nice present, or if a helpful relative pays the bill, a gift of jewelry is very suitable. The bride might give him a pair of cufflinks; he might give her a jeweled brooch. Gifts like fur coats and cars have often been exchanged among rich bridal pairs.

However, in the "real world," the gifts are often clever and not too personal or luxurious. One young woman gave her fiancé a new desk lamp for his desk, simply because she knew he needed one. Her card read, "I hope I'll always be the light of your life." He loved it. And he gave her his photograph in a handsome frame for *her* desk at the office, with a card that read, "Just to let you know I'll always be watching you, lovingly and jealously." She loved it.

The exchange of these wedding presents is usually made shortly before the wedding—the night before, for example.

How do you write a proper thank-you note for a check?

You write a letter saying "thanks for the generous check" or "the gift of stock" or whatever, but don't mention the amount.

If you have received cash, it's nice to tell the donor what you are using it for: "Now we can buy the living-room sofa." . . . "You may not know it, but if it hadn't been for your check, we never would have been able to finance a new car." People are always pleased to know what use has been made of their money gift.

I am going to have to exchange many of our wedding gifts. Do I tell the people who sent unusable or duplicate presents what I've done?

Don't tell people who sent duplicates—they'll never know as long as they can see "their" present being used in your home. Don't tell people who live far away if you've exchanged their present either. They have no way of checking.

If someone is very close to you and comes into your home often, it's better not to exchange that person's gift for something you like better. It's risking friendship over a material object. However, most people who are good friends say (or should say) to you when they give you the gift, "Now, if you don't like it, for heaven's sake, exchange it!"

If you do exchange it, you should write a warm note saying why you did it (that you "simply couldn't resist the black earthenware covered casserole that we needed so much, and I felt you would understand my predicament . . .")

We've decided to call off our wedding. Here I am sitting at home with a houseful of gifts. What do I do next?

They must be returned, and returned with a short, warm note explaining why. "We decided it was for the best to call it off, and are frankly happy we did it in time. But we are both so grateful to you for the magnificent, thoughtful gift. We return it with our love and our thanks."

The bride and her family should take care of sending back the gifts from her side of the family; the groom and his family should take care of sending back the gifts from his side. If he lives in another city, then sadly it all falls within the bride's family's responsibility.

If you're the bride, never send back your wedding gift to the store from which it came, by the way. Send it back to the donor and let him or her return it to the point of purchase.

WEDDING SHOWERS

How many wedding showers is a bride supposed to have?

Usually one is enough. It may be a combination lingerie-kitchen-bath shower, or it may be just one kind. Two showers should be maximum. A young woman who allows too many friends to entertain for her at showers is asking for criticism. People don't have enough money to keep giving present after present to a bride. The major gift should be "the wedding present" to the two of them anyway.

Who gives the shower for the bride?

Usually it's hosted by a close friend, often a member of the wedding party. The bride's closest women relatives are invited, but otherwise, it's a party for her women friends.

Should you tell people what to bring if you're giving a shower?

The shower organizer really should organize the gifts, so that duplicate presents aren't brought, and so that the bride receives what she really needs. The kitchen-shower hostess might ask one guest to bring an egg beater, another to bring a set of measuring cups; she might ask three people to go in on a good-looking wooden salad bowl with servers.

The lingerie-shower hostess should give each guest the bride's exact size and group guests together on joint gifts that are expensive, such as a nightgown with matching peignoir.

Does a bride have to write a thank-you note for each shower gift if she enthusiastically thanks each person at the party?

Yes, a thank-you note is in order for each person. A thoughtful gift (which does not have to be expensive) is in order for the shower hostess, too, as well as a very special thank-you note from the bride. Organizing a shower is a lot of work.

What about coed showers?

They are becoming more and more popular in our society, because with both people working, daytime showers for women friends are hard to organize, except on weekends. Even then, on weekends, many women don't want to be away from their husbands or male friends.

An evening cocktail-party/shower given by friends of the pair is a logical solution. Guests at the party bring joint presents to the engaged pair. The presents may be anything that the couple would use together, from bar items to kitchen items, and from bath towels to decorator pillows.

Where does the bride's trousseau come into all this shower business? Are the showers supposed to provide the trousseau?

The custom began in ancient times for a bride to bring everything needed for her new home into the marriage as her dowry. Then later the French word "trousseau" signified the clothes and lingerie that should be part of a bride's dowry. Brides collected all of these things in their "hope chests."

Today a bride brings to her marriage whatever she can— what she receives in linen or kitchen showers, and the bedding and lingerie she and her parents have purchased (which are augmented by showers and wedding gifts).

Pure linen sheets used to be the order of the day; the present world is a drip-dry one. That traditional "hope chest" simply doesn't exist. The only chest around the newlyweds' home today is usually one they found in an antique or junk shop which they use as a coffee table in their living room!

THE WEDDING SILVER

Isn't the bride supposed to supply all the sterling-silver flatware and hollowware for the marriage?

Traditionally, yes, but silver is so expensive now, many young people are "making do" with stainless until they can afford to buy it. What is interesting also is that with people marrying later than they used to, a lot of young career women are buying their own silver, piece by piece, so as to use it in entertaining long before they're married. Some of them have, by the time they marry, six dinner forks, six dinner knives, and six dessert spoons, for example, already engraved with their given-name initial or their given- and family-name initials. These initials are monogrammed straight across or vertically on the front or back of the flatware handles. Often an asterisk is included in the design. For example, Mary Brown's silver could be monogrammed M or MB.

It is still the bride's responsibility by custom to finish out the silver pattern for the marriage, but with the price of silver what it is today, whoever has the most money helps buy the silver.

How is flat silver monogrammed when combining the husband's and wife's initials?

There are several options. Let's say Mary Brown marries Andrew Fuller. The monogram combining her first-name, his first-name, and his last-name initial (F) could be done in any of these ways:

M A F   or   M A   or   F
                  F   M A

If Mary Brown's own silver was monogrammed M B before she was married, and she wants to bring Andrew into the picture, she can have the engraver add the Fuller—like this

M B
F

However, many brides when buying their wedding silver use only their maiden-name initials, having thought about the divorce rate. Sad but true.

CRYSTAL AND CHINA

My in-laws are giving us our crystal—both our good and our everyday. It's up to me to tell them what to get as our "starter"

in crystal. I would like to have eight of everything. What should I ask for?

If you want eight of everything, you had better get eleven of everything to allow for breakage. You might ask for eleven everyday water tumblers (inexpensive plain glass); eleven juice glasses (3- or 4-ounce); eleven all-purpose wineglasses; eleven old-fashioned glasses (12- to 14-ounce size are the most efficient); eleven highball glasses; and eleven cordial glasses (which may be used for everything from sherry to liqueur).

Each of these glasses is multipurpose. You can drink champagne from the wineglasses, and Irish coffee from the juice glass. You can use the highball glasses for flower vases, too, as well as using them for iced tea and beer. If someone wants a martini "straight up" and you don't have stemmed martini glasses, it's perfectly all right to serve them in the juice glasses. Wine or any cocktail served "on the rocks" may be served in the old-fashioned.

I'm confused by "place settings" in china. Do we have to buy that way? Can't we just buy so many dinner plates, salad plates, etc.? Also, can we mix patterns, or are we supposed to try for a unified china service?

You may certainly buy the separate items instead of by the place setting. Some people never use butter plates. Buy what you need and want, or list the items in the bridal registry of your local store. The same rule of logic applies here. If you want ten of everything, let us say, then buy thirteen of everything, to allow for the inevitable breakage.

You do not have to have all matched china. Some people like everything of the same pattern. Some don't. It's a question of personal taste.

BRIDAL ATTENDANTS

How are the bridesmaids chosen?

The bridesmaids are usually close friends of the bride, or relatives (including the sister of the groom if she is not a great deal older than the bride).

It is a great honor to be someone's bridesmaid, and it's usually a lot of fun, too. The bridesmaid is chosen long before the wedding, and she must order the proper dress and accessories that the bride has selected. The bridesmaids usually dress together at the same place where the bride is dressing, and they are transported to and from the church services and reception as part of the wedding party.

What's the difference between the bridesmaids and the maid of honor and matron of honor?

The maid of honor is a very close friend or perhaps the bride's sister. The matron of honor is another very close friend, one who is married (or widowed).

The maid and matron of honor see to it that the bride is properly dressed in time, and help the bride's mother with any services, small or large, that they can perform for her to make the wedding smoother. These honor attendants perform ceremonial acts during the wedding, such as holding the bride's bouquet at certain times, arranging her train every time she turns around, and handing her the ring for the groom at the right moment in a double-ring ceremony.

In a Catholic wedding, the matron of honor often lifts the bride's veil just before the "Kiss of Peace" is given in the mass.

How many bridal attendants are there supposed to be?

It depends on the size of the wedding. If several hundred are coming to the wedding, there has to be a sufficient number of ushers to seat them. (Often there are more ushers than bridesmaids for this reason.)

For a wedding planned on a very large scale, there might be eighteen attendants in all: a best man, nine other ushers, a maid of honor, a matron of honor, and six other bridesmaids.

A medium-size wedding would have a wedding party of four men and four women.

For a very small intimate wedding, such as that held for divorced pairs, a woman attendant and a man attendant are all that are necessary, and these might even be family members.

*We are starting to organize our wedding. Some of our at-
tendants are still in graduate school, and they're concerned
about how much being in the wedding is going to cost them.
We'd like a breakdown on what they're expected to pay for,
and what we, the bride and groom, should pay for.*

First of all, if you have some attendants who are really up
against it financially, arrange with some relative who can afford it to quietly pick up their expenses.

The bride's family (or whoever is paying for the wedding)
is supposed to pay all of the attendants' expenses, once they
reach the place where the wedding festivities are to be held—
and that includes lodging, all meals, transportation, etc.

The wedding party is supposed to pay its own individual
transportation expenses to and from the wedding site. The
ushers are supposed to pay for the rental of their wedding
finery, and the bridesmaids are supposed to pay for their
dresses, headdresses, and slippers.

The bridesmaids usually give a joint present to the bride—
like a sterling-silver frame for her eleven-by-fourteen formal
wedding portrait (with the wedding date engraved upon it,
and perhaps their names or facsimile signatures).

The ushers usually give a joint present to the groom, too—
like a sterling martini pitcher or bar tray or box, with the
wedding date engraved on it, his initials, and their names or
facsimile signatures.

A small wedding party would, of course, give a much more
modest gift to their bride and groom.

In 1980 I talked to one bridesmaid in a very large, fancy
wedding held in another city far away, and her total output of
expenses for her transportation, share in the bride's present,
and her wedding costume was $350. (Her transportation by
plane was $150, her dress was $100, her headdress $30, shoes
$40, and share in bride's present $30.)

In the same year I talked to a bridesmaid in a small wedding; the dresses were purchased in a modestly priced store,
and her total bill was $110. (Nothing for transportation; dress
and shoes and hairbow came to $95; participation in brides-
maids' present was $15.)

*I have three adorable nieces, ages four to twelve, and an ir-
resistible five-year-old nephew. I want very much to include
them all in my wedding, along with my six other attendants
and the groom's eight ushers. Is that all right?*

It certainly is. In European weddings, often the only attendants are the youngest members of both families. The only problem you'll have is that they're scene stealers!

Make your nephew the ring bearer. He would walk first down the aisle in the wedding procession. (Make sure also that the wedding ring is sewn into the pillow; otherwise, rest assured, no wedding ring!)

Make your two youngest nieces flower girls (they would walk next in the procession), and the twelve-year-old a junior bridesmaid. The girls' dresses should harmonize in color and theme with the bridesmaids'. (The ring bearer may wear an all-white suit or a navy jacket and navy shorts, with perhaps a white shirt with a Peter Pan collar.)

BEST MAN AND USHERS

Should I ask my brother to be my best man, or my closest friend?

Either, but it's nice to give the honor to your brother, in the spirit of the family.

Is it in order to ask my stepfather, who raised me, to be my best man?

That would be a very thoughtful gesture, one that would obviously be appreciated by him *and* your mother.

I've been asked by a fraternity brother to be his best man in a big wedding. He has gone home to prepare for the wedding, leaving me with no knowledge of what I'm to do, other than show up to get a fitting on my rented cutaway rig. What are my duties anyway?

You will have a large responsibility if the wedding is to be a big one.

For one thing, you communicate with all the ushers, to make sure they know what they're supposed to do and that they appear when they are supposed to.

You check up on whether the groom has purchased the wedding ties and gloves (if gloves are to be worn), and help him obtain the proper sizes for his ushers. You help him have his ushers' presents wrapped and ready to give out (either at the bachelor dinner or at the rehearsal dinner).

You make sure the groom has ordered the boutonnieres for all the men and that the bride's bouquet is taken care of.

You coordinate with the bride's parents the handling of the cars and limousines that will transport everyone to and from the parties, the church service, the reception, etc.

You round up the ushers for the wedding rehearsal and make sure they know what their duties are in seating the guests and how to perform their other responsibilities.

You lead off the toasts at the bridal dinner and at the wedding reception, too—toasting the bride first. You make sure all the other people who should be toasted *are* toasted (the grandmother of the bride, etc.).

You get the groom dressed and to the church on time, with the wedding ring in your own vest pocket and the wedding license in the groom's inside pocket. You are a witness of the signing of the wedding certificate, along with one of the bride's attendants.

You carry the clergyman's fee and the church fee in envelopes in your pocket.

You take charge of the couple's luggage and transportation for their getaway from the reception.

You help solve all problems and divert all emergencies!

If the best man does all that, what is there left for the ushers to do?

The ushers have a very important role to play in the wedding. First of all, they should make sure that all of the bridesmaids and the bride's honor attendants have a great time at the wedding. Second, they are in charge of seating all the wedding guests—each usher giving his arm to each woman guest and escorting her down the aisle, her husband or escort or children bringing up the rear. He should seat the bride's friends on the left, the groom's on the right, except when there is a very lopsided situation, such as occurs when the groom comes from another part of the country. In this case, the ushers should even up the number of guests on each side.

If more than two women in one family appear at once, the usher should escort the older woman down the aisle, leaving the younger woman to get to her seat on her own.

Five minutes before the bride's mother is seated, an usher

should escort the mother of the groom to her place in the first row on the right.

Then the bride's mother is taken down the aisle and she is seated with other members of her party in the first row on the left.

This is the signal for the wedding procession to begin.

The ushers will be rehearsed before the wedding on how they go down the aisle, what they do during the service, and how they escort the bridal attendants from the church at the end. They are also supposed to help assure a successful wedding reception at which everyone has a good time without becoming rowdy.

A wedding reception should be a great, memorable party, but it doesn't have to be an undignified one!

BACHELOR DINNER

In a moment of weakness I promised my college roommate that I'd organize a bachelor dinner for him before the wedding. Now that I've promised, and since I've never attended one before, I need some suggestions.

The male side of the wedding party, groom included, is supposed to be in good shape for the wedding, and not suffering from a mass state of advanced hangovers. This is why bachelor dinners are not held as often as they used to be. The proverbial drunken brawl with a chorus girl leaping from a giant cake has fortunately become a relic of the not-too-distant past. Today's bachelor dinners can be sane affairs, and since you'll be organizing the party, you can keep it from becoming too rowdy.

The dinner is held usually two or three nights previous to the wedding, often in a club or the private dining room of a restaurant. It is often dutch treat (except for the groom's share, of course). Sometimes the bride dines with her bridal attendants the same night, somewhere else.

The groom may wish to present his ushers with their ushers' gifts at his bachelor dinner, and they in turn may wish to give him their special gift.

Properly organized, it is an evening of sentimental toasting, a lot of good-natured teasing, and the retelling of tales among good male friends.

A tip: keep the cocktail hour short before dinner. Then

break up the party at a decent hour, like eleven, and make everyone head for home.

THE REHEARSAL DINNER

What is the scenario for the rehearsal dinner, and who gives it?

If the wedding is on a Saturday, for example, then a rehearsal of the ceremony is usually held on Friday afternoon around four o'clock, in the church or wherever the service is to be held. Then a dinner, traditionally given by the groom's parents, often follows. (If the bride's family can afford this expense and the groom's can't, the bride's family hosts the dinner.)

Guests include the wedding party, their spouses, and close family and friends. If the clergyman and his or her spouse are good friends, they should also be included.

The party can be formal, like a sit-down dinner in a club, or informal, like a barbecue in the backyard. It is often the party the wedding attendants enjoy the most during the weekend.

My brother and sister-in-law are deceased. As the groom's aunt, I would like to do as they would have done, and host the rehearsal dinner. Is this all right for me to do?

It would be very nice of you. If the parents of the groom, for one reason or another, are unable to host the dinner, any relative or close friend my step in to do the honors.

How is the toasting handled at a rehearsal dinner?

The best man, early in the dinner, should lead off the toasting. He makes a toast to the bride in a light and amusing tone, but his toast should also be complimentary. Humorous insults at a time like this are remembered long afterward more for their insults than for their humor.

The bride answers the toast with one to her groom. The groom then answers with one to the mother of the bride. The father of the groom might then toast the bride, and the father of the bride might toast the parents of the groom—and so on, until finally every member of the immediate families has been taken care of in the toasting.

If the best man assigns toasts beforehand to everyone, it all works much more smoothly and easily. For example, the bride's young brother could be asked to toast his grandmother, and one of the bridesmaids could salute the groom's little sister, etc.

THE BRIDE'S DRESS

What's the difference between a formal and an informal wedding dress?

A formal wedding dress, which may be worn in a church, home, club, or hotel wedding, is full-length, either all-white, off-white, or a very pale pastel. For a traditional formal wedding, the sleeves are long, or if they are short, the bride may wear long white kid gloves. The neckline is a modest one. The gown may have a long cathedral train; a fingertip veil is usually worn, often trimmed in lace and held to the head by means of some kind of band or cap.

Her matching silk or satin slippers should be "broken in" around the house long before the wedding. A bride with sore feet has a difficult time looking "radiant"!

An informal gown may be short, three-quarter-length, or to the floor. It is white, off-white, or pale pastel. The bride may wear a veil if she wishes.

I've been married before, but it was an elopement. Now I'm being married again, and I want to wear the white wedding dress I have always longed for. Under these circumstances, it is all right to be married in white, isn't it?

You would feel and look better wearing a cream-colored or pastel floor-length dress, without a veil. You might wear a pastel printed chiffon or any soft and pretty dress that is not "bridal white."

The smart thing for a woman to do when selecting a dress for her second or third marriage is to pick a dress she would enjoy wearing time and time again as a late-afternoon or evening dress.

What do you do with a formal white wedding dress? Can you restyle it so it can be worn again?

Some wedding dresses lend themselves to transformations into evening gowns. However, an exquisite formal wedding dress should really be cleaned and laid carefully away in layers of tissue paper in a well-labeled and sturdy box—to await the future brides of this and later generations who will want to wear it in their weddings.

I am a bride-to-be of fifty-four. I obviously can't wear a long white dress. Yet I deserve to wear white. What would be appropriate? I don't want anyone saying as I walk down the aisle, "There goes the old fool!"

Wear a long white crepe dinner gown, or a white "garden-party" dress. A white silk suit with matching hat would look very smart, if your wedding is small. And a long white "theater suit" would be very appropriate, too.

BRIDAL PORTRAIT

When should the bride's formal wedding portrait be taken?

After the final fitting of her gown, when the veil or headdress is complete, and when her hair has been done perfectly (and in the style which she will wear on her wedding day).

How do we get our daughter's wedding picture into the paper?

Often the photographer who takes the formal portrait will submit an eight-by-ten glossy photo (black and white) of the bride's choice to the paper's society department. The family may also submit the photograph, with all the proper information on the wedding attached. Be sure to check with the editor on how much time is required in order to get the photograph into the Sunday papers (or whatever date you wish the picture and story to run). You must also figure into your calculations the time needed by the photographer to develop the film and to process the prints.

Relatives and members of the wedding party are asking for a free print of our daughter's wedding portrait. Are we supposed to oblige them? It would break the bank!

You should present one to the groom's family, give one to the bride and groom, and keep one for yourself. Tell all the others who ask that there will be some excellent candids taken at the wedding and that you will see to it that they each of them has a good photograph of the bride and groom as a memento.

What kind of makeup should I use for my wedding photograph? I don't want it to look dated in the coming years.

Use a pale-colored lipstick, and don't overload the eyes with mascara and eyeliner. Soft, natural-looking makeup is *never* dated. A bride, wearing the "latest thing" in makeup fads in her photograph, a few years hence might look as dated as Clara Bow does to us now with her "cupid's mouth" of the twenties.

THE RINGS AND JEWELRY

What does the bride do with her engagement ring when she gets married? Isn't the lowest ring on the wedding finger supposed to be the wedding ring? In the ceremony, does the groom have to remove the engagement ring before he puts the wedding ring on her finger?

The bride should switch her engagement ring to her right hand before the ceremony. She can switch it back later, putting it above her wedding ring.

What kind of jewelry should I wear on my wedding day? I have a lot, and I'd like to wear it, because my formal wedding dress is so very plain.

It's better to control the urge to wear all your jewelry with your wedding dress. Something in diamonds and pearls is appropriate, but not too much. A pearl necklace or a small one with diamonds, one diamond or pearl bracelet, and earrings of pearls or of pearls and diamonds are in order.

In a double-ring ceremony, who orders the groom's ring and has it engraved?

The bride or her family takes care of the expense and the ordering. The engraving should be the same as that in her own ring (often just the pair of initials and the date).

The groom's wedding ring may or may not match the bride's. Sometimes the groom will wear a wedding ring for the ceremony only, as a symbolic gesture.

I have a small diamond engagement ring and a gold wedding band. My grandmother has just given me as a wedding present two sapphire bands she calls "guard rings." I don't know how to group all the rings on the third finger of my left hand.

Place your wedding ring on the finger first, then one sapphire guard ring, then your diamond engagement ring, then the other sapphire guard ring.

I have two pieces of advice for brides and their rings: Keep them clean and keep them insured!

OTHERS IN THE WEDDING

Are the maid and matron of honor supposed to be dressed differently from the other bridesmaids?

Sometimes they are dressed identically. Sometimes only their flower headdresses are different. Sometimes they wear the same dresses as the bridesmaids, but in a different color.

Is the junior bridesmaid dressed the same way the older women are?

Yes, unless she would look silly in something like a bridesmaid's off-the-shoulder Scarlett O'Hara dress. She should look dressed for her age, but often the same dress the others are wearing would look well on her—perhaps in a shorter length, or perhaps with short sleeves or a higher neck.

May the flower girl wear just her regular party dress? I don't feel like buying a new dress for my daughter for a two-minute appearance down the church aisle.

Yes, if her party dress matches the feeling of the bridesmaids' attire, she may certainly wear it. Her costume can be
tied into the others' by wearing the same flowers in her hair.

*As the bride's mother (and I'll pass this information on to the
groom's mother, too), I would like to know what to wear if
our children are married at a formal evening ceremony. Also,
what would we wear if the children decide on an afternoon
wedding instead?*

For the formal evening wedding, each of you would wear a
floor-length evening gown, not too décolleté, with evening
slippers and bag. If your gown has short sleeves, you could
wear long white gloves if you wish. If it's cold weather, wear
a fur. (If you don't own one, it's the time to borrow one.)

If the couple marries in the afternoon, you may wear a very
simple long-length or three-quarter-length covered-up dress.
In other words, a dinner gown or a dressy cocktail dress is
appropriate.

An afternoon wedding calls for a minimum, not a maximum, of jewelry.

*If I'm thirty-eight years old and getting married for the first
time, may I wear a long formal white wedding gown?*

It's your constitutional right, but I think you'd feel better if
you wore a white gown that is not a formal wedding dress,
but more of an evening gown. Work out with a milliner or
your hairdresser a small white hat with a veil or a simple white
headpiece (some tiny flowers anchored to a white velvet
bandeau, for example).

*Are there any hard-and-fast rules governing how women
guests dress at weddings?*

Nothing hard-and-fast, but some pretty logical ones. For
example, don't wear black (symbol of mourning), and don't
wear a fancy white dress (people will think you're competing
with the bride). Don't be too décolleté, particularly if you
attend the church service, and don't wear glittery fabrics like
gold lamé before a six-o'clock wedding. Easy on the jewelry,
too. The show is supposed to be the bride's, not yours.

Is it all right for me to wear an evening dress to a friend's wedding at four o'clock? Someone told me that was wrong.

At Christian weddings, guests don't come in evening dress unless the invitation is for services at six or after and the words "black tie" are written on it. You'd feel embarrassed in a long gown under the circumstances.

FLOWERS FOR THE WEDDING PARTY

What's the best flower for the groom's boutonniere? Do his ushers wear the exact same thing?

Any small pretty flower or cluster of tiny flowers is appropriate for the groom. It's nice if it's something from his bride's bouquet. The ushers and his best man would wear *another* kind of boutonniere, not a matching one.

Do the bridesmaids carry flowers that are different from the bride's bouquet?

Yes. The bride may carry an all-white bouquet or one that is mixed with pastel flowers. The bride may wish to carry instead a white Bible or prayer book, trailing white satin streamers intertwined with flowers like orchids.

The bridal attendants may carry either bouquets (equipped with hand holders), or sheaves of flowers, cradled into their arms and tied with ribbon. Florists are becoming more creative today in coming up with new ideas for the bride's and the bridesmaids' flowers.

Do the mothers of the bride and groom have to wear corsages?

No. Women who don't like to wear corsages can eschew them.

THE MALE WEDDING-PARTY ATTIRE

Who decides what the men in the wedding will wear?

Once the bride decides what she will wear, the groom has a choice of rather limited options for the men. He really should adhere to the bride's family's preference on what he and his ushers should wear. If the wedding is in winter and is a formal one, all the men should be formally dressed, too.

For example, for a formal evening wedding, the groom would wear a full-dress tailcoat with a white waistcoat, a starched shirt with a wing collar, and a white piqué or waffle-weave tie. He would wear studs (no colored stones, please), black patent shoes, and dress socks. His ushers and the fathers of bride and groom would dress the same.

For a formal daytime wedding, the men might wear black or oxford-gray cutaways or long jackets with gray vests and gray striped trousers. The cutaway calls for a wing-collar shirt with an ascot; the long jacket calls for a starched fold collar or a regular broadcloth shirt with French cuffs and a four-in-hand tie. Black shoes and socks are the order of the day.

Trousers should break slightly about the top of the shoe; the jacket collar should hug the neck, and at least a half inch of white cuffs should show beneath the jacket sleeve.

An informal evening wedding is simple: black tie. A black dinner suit (or a white dinner jacket with black trousers in summer) is very appropriate. Black ties and cummerbunds should be worn, as well as black patent shoes and socks.

For an informal wedding held before six o'clock, all-white suits or white or gray flannel trousers worn with dark blazers are the best. These are worn with white shirts and four-in-hand ties.

Colorful wedding attire or suits with colored piping, worn with ruffed shirts, are popular in many parts of the country, but if you want to know what always looks *just right*, stick to blacks and grays and not colored suits. And forget the piping and frilly shirts. (A personal opinion!)

The men's rented attire should be arranged for at least a month in advance, to allow for alterations. This requires the groom and the best man to be conscientious about getting everyone to the rental place in time.

The groom buys his ushers their ties and also their gloves, if gloves are to be worn at the formal ceremony.

What are male wedding guests supposed to wear?

Dark business suits in the winter, dark lightweight suits in the summer, or any solid conservative-colored summer suits. The ties are preferably conservative, too.

If it's a black-tie evening wedding, men guests wear black tie, too. If a man is a relative of the bride or groom and the wedding is a formal white-tie-and-tails affair, he has the privilege of wearing one, too, although the other guests would wear black dinner suits.

WEDDING PROTOCOL

What's the order for a Christian procession into the church?

For a Christian processional the bridegroom, the best man, and the clergyman are already in the church, waiting at the chancel steps when the wedding march begins. From the back of the church the ushers walk first (in pairs, shortest first, tallest last). Then come the ring bearer, flower girl, and junior bridesmaids (if there are any), followed by the bridesmaids (often in pairs, the shorter ones first). Then come the maid and the matron of honor, and finally the bride on the arm of her father (or whoever is giving her away).

If there are any pages (these are preschool children used only for the most formal of weddings, as is the custom seen in many Latin and European countries), they follow last, carrying—more or less efficiently!—the bride's train.

What's the order in a Jewish wedding?

For an orthodox Jewish processional, for example, the rabbi walks first (but not if the ceremony takes place in a temple or synagogue). He is followed by the best man, then the groom —flanked by his mother and father. They in turn are followed by the maid or matron of honor, then the flower girl or page (if any), and finally the bride, flanked by her mother on her right and her father on her left.

What is the proper form for the wedding party to use in leaving the church when the wedding is over?

In a Christian recessional, the bride takes the groom's arm and they lead. They are followed by the matron of honor with the best man (or the maid of honor with the best man, if there is no matron).

Then the other attendants walk out, men and women paired, the shortest first, the tallest last.

If there are any children involved, such as a ring bearer and flower girl, they walk in between the honor attendants and the other bridal attendants. Many a ring bearer by now has had enough of trying to be quiet during the festivities, and he may need a helping hand from one of the bridesmaids.

In an orthodox Jewish recessional the bride and groom walk first, followed by the bride's parents, the groom's parents, then the maid or matron of honor with the best man, and finally the rabbi.

Sometimes the attendants, in pairs, precede the rabbi and form a guard of honor through which the rest of the procession walks.

In the processional, which of her father's arms is the bride supposed to take going down the aisle?

Either side is all right. The clergyman may have a preference himself. When the bride goes down on her father's left arm, she's on the arm "nearest his heart." But when she goes down on his right arm, it's often simpler. Her father has to step back when he gives her away and return to his pew on the left side of the church. Many a father has tripped on his daughter's train when crossing over from her right side back to his pew on the left side.

We have two main aisles in our church. Which one should we use for the wedding?

Why not use them both—one for the processional, one for the recessional?

My father is handicapped. Can he still give me away at my wedding?

Definitely, yes. It's done all the time. If there's a wheelchair involved or any problem of movement, ask your clergyman exactly how he prefers to do it.

My father isn't living. Who should give me away?

Whether a bride's father is deceased, or just absent, someone else may do the honors for her.

Your brother, a male cousin, an uncle, a grandfather, or even a male relative or close friend of the groom's family may appropriately bring you down the aisle.

I am a fifty-year-old bride. Who should give me away?

You may dispense with this part of the ceremony. If you are having a very small wedding, wait with the groom and your two attendants in the vestry until the clergyman is ready for the ceremony to begin. The groom's attendant would escort you to the chancel, and your groom would escort your maid or matron of honor to the chancel behind you.

What happens at the altar? What does everyone do?

Once the wedding party is in place, different rituals are performed in Protestant, Catholic, and Jewish ceremonies. Ask your clergyman and he will inform you of each step each member of the wedding party goes through.

When does the groom kiss the bride?

At large formal church weddings a kiss is not part of the ceremony, but it often takes place at the altar after the groom and bride have been congratulated by the clergyman. If she is wearing a veil, her maid or matron of honor should lift the veil for her, but sometimes the groom does it.

At informal weddings, the kiss usually takes place right after the couple has received the clergyman's congratulations.

In Catholic weddings, after the "Kiss of Peace" part of the mass, the couple often proceeds to the front pews, to kiss both sets of parents and relatives.

DOUBLE WEDDINGS

My younger sister and I (younger by one year only) are planning a double wedding. We have the same friends, so our bridesmaids, except for our separate maids of honor, will be

*the same. The ushers for the two grooms will be different.
How do we handle this? Who goes down the aisle first, gets
married first, and who goes down the aisle on our father's
arm?*

You, as the older daughter, take precedence. You are the
one who goes down the aisle on your father's arm. Your
sister would be escorted by a brother or an uncle or some
close male relative or friend.

Your sister's attendants, your sister, and the man escorting
her would precede your attendants, and you with your father.
(If your attendants are the same, divide them with your
sister.)

As the older sister, you would be married by the clergyman
first, and in the recessional, you and your husband would be
the first couple out the door.

If there are two main aisles in the church, your sister should
use one, and you the other.

*We're having a double wedding. I want my bridesmaids'
dresses totally different from my cousin's, and my fiancé
wants his ushers dressed differently, too. Is that all right?*

Yes and no. The two sets of bridesmaids' dresses may be
different, but should not be so contrasting that it looks terrible
at the altar. The ushers for both grooms *must* be dressed
the same, however. They are out in the church seating people for a long time before the ceremony, and it would not
look right to have them dressed in two separate styles.

*For our double wedding, should we have one huge cake or
two separate ones?*

Separate ones, by all means, if that is what you'd prefer.

WEDDINGS AT HOME

*If you're having a home wedding, do you provide seats for
the ceremony?*

If the ceremony will last longer than ten minutes, there
should be seats provided. If there are quite a few guests expected, rope off a section on either side of the altar—the left

side (facing the altar) for the bride's family, the right side
for the groom's.

*I'm being married at home. Our house is quite small and it
will hold a maximum of about twenty guests. I would like
to wear a long formal white gown and veil. Is this proper?*

Proper, yes, but you'd be a much more comfortable bride
in that small space if you wore a simple long gown or a three-
quater-length one without a veil. A bride in a full formal
gown with all the trappings needs a lot of room in which to
maneuver!

*My brother wants to play his guitar at our wedding at home.
I don't want him playing at the wedding, because I want our
church organist to play traditional wedding music on the
small electric organ we have. I really want traditional music,
but my brother is insistent, and the family is in an uproar.
How would you settle this one?*

The case of the relative who wants to play or sing in the
wedding is a commonplace problem. To keep peace, a compromise is usually best.

In your case, why don't you let your brother play his
guitar softly in the front, in one corner, facing the guests as
they take their seats before the service starts? Then, the minute the processional begins, he can sit down with the family
while the organist takes over.

*When the wedding service at home is over, do we all pro-
ceed to a place where we begin a receiving line to greet our
guests?*

If yours is a small wedding in a small house, you would not
need a receiving line. Instead, after the service, you would
greet each guest informally and then proceed with them
to the area where the food and drink are being served.

If the guest list is sizable and your house is ample, or if
you plan to ask more people to the wedding reception than
are invited to the service, you should form a receiving line.
Place yourselves in an area that has an entrance and an

exit—like a small room near the main room. Try to avoid a traffic jam of people.

We might have a judge marry us at home. He's a friend of the family's. What kind of fee do we give him?

He probably would not accept a fee. It's more suitable to send him a gift later—anything from two seats to the local professional football game to a case of liquor.

Be sure that the judge and his or her spouse are honored guests at your reception.

CIVIL CEREMONIES

We are being married in a civil ceremony in the judge's chambers. How do we dress? Do we give the judge money? How many attendants may we have?

For a civil marriage in a registrar's office or in the judge's chambers, the bride would wear a simple dress or suit—never a wedding gown. She may carry flowers, a white Bible, or a prayer book if she wishes (and with something festive like a flowered ribbon marker in it). She may want to wear a smart hat and gloves with her costume.

The groom would wear a dark business suit and a conservative tie. Each would have an attendant, and these attendants would act as the couple's witnesses, too.

The best man hands the presiding official a sealed envelope containing the fee before the ceremony (this may be $10, $25, $50, or more, according to the circumstances).

No fee is given when a high-ranking official, such as the mayor or the governor, performs the ceremony; one might send him or her a present afterward, however.

THE RECEPTION

What's the best way to move the wedding party from the church to the reception?

The easiest way, of course, is by limousines. But these are not on everyone's budget. The best man should arrange, long before the wedding, the number of friends required to volunteer themselves and their cars to transport the wedding party to the church and then to the reception.

One thing everyone should remember is that the bride and groom should have the backseat of their car to themselves on the way to the reception. A little privacy is cherished at this moment in their lives—even if all they have to say to each other at that moment is "Good Lord, my feet hurt!"

When are the group photographs taken of the couple, their attendants, and their parents?

Usually the easiest and most efficient place to do it is at the reception, the minute everyone arrives. The wedding guests usually dawdle in arriving at the reception after the church services, so this is the time to get the groupings together and let the photographer do his job.

A nice background should be chosen—perhaps the area in which the receiving line will be formed, which might be banked in flowers. The best man and the maid of honor should work hard to pull everyone together quickly.

What's the order for the receiving line?

The bride's mother stands first, since she is the hostess. Next comes the groom's mother, and then, optionally, the bride's father, if he wants to be in the receiving line (many do not).

Next come the bride, the groom, the matron or maid of honor, and the bridesmaids. (The children—very junior bridesmaids, flower girls, pages—do not have to stand in this line, because it would bore them *very* quickly.)

If the groom's father stands in the receiving line at a very formal wedding reception, he would stand between the bride's mother and his own wife.

Is the bridal party allowed to drink in the receiving line, and are the guests allowed to go through the line with drinks in their hands?

Those in the receiving line are not supposed to have glasses in their hands. However, their ushers and nice friends usually keep them supplied with glasses of champagne on the table or mantel behind them. Everyone can surreptitiously turn around and take a sip from time to time.

The guests are not supposed to have a glass in hand as they go through the line. Often there's such a long wait to go through the receiving line they help themselves from a passing tray, but when they arrive at the bridal party's position, they should put their glasses down somewhere, and return to them after greeting the wedding party.

My mother is dead. Is it all right for my father to be the first in line to greet the guests in her place?

Yes, he certainly may. He may also ask a close female relative, like his sister, to stand with him to help receive the guests.

My parents are divorced and my father is remarried. My father is giving us the reception. I'm a little confused as to who stands in the receiving line.

Your mother would stand first, and your father next to her —as a salute to their daughter's happiness, no matter how much bitterness there may be between them.

Your father's present wife would attend the reception as a guest, and would not stand in the receiving line.

I'm always tongue-tied going down the receiving line. I never know what to say to anyone.

Fortunately for you, it's not a time for long orations. No one should talk too long, or a jam-up occurs. Shake warmly the hand of everyone you meet, and give your own name. "I'm Sally King" (not "Mrs. John King"). Smile a lot, and tell the parents of the bride and groom what a beautiful, stunning wedding it was. Tell the bride she looks truly beautiful. Congratulate both of them and say something like "I wish you all the happiness in the world." As for the bridesmaids, if you don't know them, just smile, give your name, shake their hands, and say, "Nice wedding," or "Glad to meet you." The faster you move through the line, the better for everyone.

As for the bride and groom, about all they can mutter is "Thank you so much" to all the compliments and best wishes. They may also slip in a "Glad you were with us today," or to an older person close to the family, "It meant a lot to us to have you here."

The groom will find himself spending most of his time agreeing that, yes, his bride is truly lovely, and, yes he *is* a lucky man.

The receiving line has to practice ungluing the smiles on their faces after about fifteen minutes. By the end of a long, long receiving line they are usually ready to say nothing to anyone, to kick off their shoes, and to be antisocial for a few minutes.

Are there any special instructions for the photographer at the reception?

Someone—one of the bride's parents or the best man or the maid of honor—should hand the photographer a list of every relative and member of the wedding party and then point out each person, so that a good candid will be made of each one.

The photographer should also be given a list of shots that are "musts"—*e.g.*, a number of shots of the receiving line, one of the cake-cutting ceremony, the bride dancing with her father, with the groom, the groom dancing with the flower girl, etc. The photographer should be on the spot when the bride tosses her bouquet at the bridesmaids (and also her garter at the ushers, if that's part of the action). The photographer should capture the good-bye scene with the parents and the newlyweds' departure in the car.

Most wedding photographers know what scenes to take, but someone should be assigned to help sort out the leading cast of characters.

What kind of a budget should we allow for flowers at the reception? We are counting pennies at this moment.

Then don't overdo the reception flowers. Tell the florist to use more greenery than flowers. You might use the plants you have in your own home, too. Don't worry about decorating the entire area with flowers. The people, the food, the cake, and the festive spirit will provide sufficient decoration as it is.

Where do the members of the bridal party sit at the reception?

At a large formal reception there is often a bride's table, decorated with white flowers and with the tiered wedding cake as the centerpiece. There are place cards telling the members of the wedding party where to sit (their spouses usually do not sit at this table). The bride and groom sit in the center (the bride on the groom's right). The best man sits to her right; the maid or matron of honor sits to the groom's left.

Even if the wedding reception is buffet-style, the bridal table is served by a waiter or waitress.

Where do the parents of the couple sit at a formal reception?

A special table may be planned for them, too, if it's a wedding breakfast or supper. Place cards are used on this table, too, with the bride's mother acting as hostess, with the groom's father on her right; opposite her is her husband, with the groom's mother on his right, and so on. The grandparents of the couple, the clergyman and his or her spouse, and any distinguished guests (such as the mayor, a congressman, a university president) would be included at that table.

When is the wedding cake cut and where should it be placed if you don't have a bride's table?

The wedding cake should have its own white-covered table, prettily decorated in greenery. At a certain moment, if there is music, the song "The Bride Cuts the Cake" is played, people stop dancing, and everyone should cluster around for the ceremony.

A silver cake knife is used; the handle may be decorated with white satin streamers and flowers. The pair cuts the first slice together; they share the eating of it, and then the

headwaiter (or a member of the family at a small wedding)
finishes the slicing of the cake and passing it to all the guests.

The cake may be made of anything, but its frosting must
be white (although pastel flowers may be part of the decoration).

Nothing should be "written" on the icing, by the way.

*We plan to have a four-piece band at the wedding reception.
When do people start dancing? Do they have to wait for the
bride and groom?*

If it's a small wedding, no one starts dancing until the
bride and groom have had their first dance. If it's a big wedding, the long receiving line will take a long time, so the
guests begin to dance immediately.

When the receiving line finally breaks up, the groom leads
the bride onto the floor, and they traditionally do a waltz,
with the floor cleared and with everyone watching and
clapping.

This is a short dance because the newlyweds are usually
embarrassed; in a matter of two minutes the bride's father
and mother might begin to dance, then the parents of the
groom and the other members of the wedding party. Finally
the guests join the group. The father of the bride should cut
in on his daughter; so should the father of the groom; then
the best man; and all the ushers. Wedding guests may also
cut in at this point.

When does the wedding reception end?

After the bride throws her bouquet (and garter), she and
the groom go to separate quarters to dress for their honeymoon trip, assisted by their wedding attendants.

When they come to the front door, they say good-bye to
everyone and depart in a shower of rice or flower petals or
confetti. The remaining wedding guests may go on dancing
for a few minutes, but they should really depart at this point.

*I am the hostess in my own small apartment for our wedding
reception. What kind of food should I serve?*

The easiest is to serve wine (or champagne, if you can afford it) and hors d'oeuvres, either before lunch or from five to seven in the evening. Have a wedding cake, of course. Some of your friends might volunteer to make the hors d'oeuvres for you and bring them to your apartment. Someone should also clean up for you after you have gone on your wedding trip. That's what friends are for.

My parents are going to give me a wedding breakfast after our wedding mass. We're all a little confused about what the food should be.

A wedding breakfast is really lunch—three courses, served either buffet-style or seated.

There should be a simple first course, then an easy-to-serve main dish, like beef Stroganoff or a spicy creamed turkey with rice or noodles and a salad; and then perhaps a fancy ice-cream mold to go with the wedding cake.

You would serve wine through the "breakfast" and champagne with the cake, or perhaps champagne all the way through, if you can afford it.

SECOND AND THEREAFTER MARRIAGES

I am marrying a divorcée. Since I haven't been married before, I'd like to have a bachelor dinner. We'd also like to have a large group of friends in the church, as well as at the reception. In this way I can invite eight or nine ushers to be in the wedding. Is this all right?

If the bride is being married for the first time, the groom may have a bachelor dinner, the wedding in the church may be a major event, and all stops may be pulled. But if the bride is being married for the second or third time, everything changes. The religious ceremony should be simple and attended by only close friends and family. The reception may be as large as the couple wishes.

Therefore, go ahead and have a small, quiet bachelor dinner, but make it a group of your close male friends. They will not be ushers, because with a small, simple wedding service with few people present, ushers are not needed.

It's an unfair situation, really. If the bride has been married before, and the groom hasn't, the groom is deprived of being able to participate in the segments of a major wedding. But if the groom has been married before and the bride has not, the wedding may be as big and fancy as desired.

My daughter is being married for the second time, at the age of twenty-four. Do we announce her engagement with a party and with information sent to the society section of our local newspapers?

No, engagements are not formally announced when it's the woman's second marriage. (If it's her groom-to-be's second wedding and her first, however, a formal engagement party is in order.)

Your daughter should either call or write to her family and close friends to tell them of her happy news.

What kind of invitation does a widow or divorcée send for her small second wedding?

She could telephone the invitations or send a Mailgram or a brief note, such as this one:

Dear Aunt Anne,

Stephen and I have set the date—Saturday, April 5, at the Chapel of the Seafarer, five o'clock. We're having everyone come after the ceremony for some champagne and a buffet supper at the Cape Cod Room in the Tollhouse Inn.

You *must* be there. We can't get married without you!

Love,
Judy

Our daughter and future son-in-law want a large reception after their wedding ceremony. Both have been married before, but they are young and their first marriages were quick mistakes. They want to invite all their close friends and "do it up right," which neither did in their first marriages. It is proper to send out engraved reception invitations?

Absolutely. A reception invitation like yours may be handwritten on paper, or written by a calligrapher on special stock, or you may have it printed or engraved. The text might read like this, if you, the parents, are extending the invitations:

Mr. and Mrs. Hugh Ridings Knowlton
request the pleasure of your company
at the wedding reception of their daughter
Mrs. Alexandra Knowlton Shaw
and
Mr. Malcolm Baldwin Reynolds
on Saturday, May 6
at five-thirty o'clock
Beverly Wilshire Hotel
Beverly Hills

RSVP
1624 Canyon Drive
La Canada, California zip code

I would like the announcement of my second marriage to be in our local newspaper. How should I do it?

Two weeks before the marriage, you should submit to your local society editor some typed copy with a "Hold for release for such and such a date" (the date you should use is the day *after* your wedding). Here is a typical announcement:

Hold for Release October 4

Mrs. Abigail Adler Sundlun and Mr. Gordon Leon Fuller, both of Omaha, Nebraska, were married here Sunday, October third, in the Fontanelle Hotel by Judge Walker Wright of the Nebraska State Supreme Court. Mrs. Fuller is the daughter of Mr. and Mrs. Edward Adler, Jr., of Chicago. She is a lawyer with the firm of Sundlun and Frazier. Mr. Fuller is the son of Mrs. John Anthony Fuller and the late Mr. Fuller of Council Bluffs, Iowa. He is president the Red Arrow Foodstuffs Corporation. Mr. and Mrs. Fuller each have two children from their previous marriages, which were terminated by divorce. The couple will continue to reside in Omaha.

Is it proper for my children to attend their father's upcoming wedding? I don't want them to go, but someone told me I was being selfish and that I would be criticized by our friends for not letting them attend. Their father even wants our oldest teenage son to be his attendant.

If the children are close to their father, the nicest thing for you to do is to urge them to attend and allow your son to serve as his father's attendant with your blessing. Your children are going to know this is a very tough situation for you, and they are going to respect you greatly for your lack of acrimony and selfishness.

It might be your natural inclination to say to your children, "If you have any love for me, you won't go to the wedding of your father to that 'other woman.' "

It takes strength to say to your children, "This is all very hard on me, but I want to keep the remnants of our family together; it will mean a great deal to your father to have you there, so go."

Who pays for the second wedding?

It depends. If the bride is a young widow or divorcée, her parents might pay for everything again. If both bride and groom are mature and working, they would pay for it themselves. If either the bride or the groom is well-off and the other one is not, the one who can afford it would pay for it.

Wedding Anniversaries

We are going to have a black-tie dinner dance in honor of our parents' fiftieth wedding anniversary. We also insist on the "no-presents-are-to-be-brought" aspect. There are five of us giving this party, but the eldest daughter will collect and keep track of the acceptances and regrets. Will you help us word the invitations?

A formal engraved or printed invitation might look like this:

In honour of
the fiftieth wedding anniversary of
Mr. and Mrs. Roland Howard Smith
their sons and daughters
request the pleasure of your company
at a dinner-dance
on Friday, the fifth of February
at seven o'clock
The Fox Chapel Golf Club
Fox Chapel

Black Tie
No gifts please

RSVP
Mrs. Johnson Garrett
3455 Inverness Street
Pittsburgh, Pennsylvania zip code

*What are some of the nice things we can do for our parents'
Golden Anniversary party, which they are hosting themselves?*

You should organize some clever and sentimental toasts.
If you are going to sing songs with special lyrics, practice
them diligently beforehand.

Tape all the proceedings, so that your parents can replay
it whenever they wish. Have a photographer record everything. Have as close a replica as possible of their original
wedding cake for them to cut together. You might decorate
the walls of the room where the party is to be held with
blow-ups of their old wedding photographs borrowed from
family albums.

*What kind of twenty-fifth anniversary present does one give
a couple who has everything?*

Since the twenty-fifth is symbolically sterling silver, it
might be too expensive to follow tradition and to give a
gift of sterling—particularly since the couple may have all the
silver they want and need by now anyway. Be creative about
your gift.

You might order something commemorative in crystal, like

a bowl or a set of bar glasses, with their initials and "25th" etched into the glass.

A leather photo album, to house all the photos to be taken at the anniversary party, and marked in silver on the cover with the couple's initials and "The 25th" would make a nice gift. One person I know had cocktail napkins printed—a year's supply—with the phrase "Twenty-five years and going strong." Another presented twenty-five tiny green plants in clay pots to the couple on their anniversary, with a note that stated, "Twenty-five years of growing love are symbolized in this gift." The plants cost a dollar each; they were worth a great deal more to the couple, who referred to them thereafter as "our anniversary plants."

We are celebrating our thirty-fifth anniversary and wish to repeat our wedding. I would like to wear my wedding dress, which still fits. How do we communicate on the invitations that we are holding our wedding again?

It's better not to refer to it as a repetition of a wedding. You can't be "married again" unless you were divorced and wish to remarry.

Instead, why don't you invite your family and friends to "a reaffirmation of our marriage vows" at a regularly scheduled service (for which the clergyman has agreed to repeat the vows). A luncheon could follow. You would dress in a nice dress and your husband in a business suit (not wedding clothes).

No one would stand up for you as attendants, because it's not a wedding, but you could put wedding rings on each other's fingers at the renewal of your vows. If your rings are old and battered, you might have new ones for the occasion.

Funerals

I want to leave my affairs in proper order for my wife and children. A friend of mine died recently, and since he was not properly organized, his estate is tied up and his family is in dire straits. I don't wish this to happen to mine.

Every person should have a file marked "To be opened in case of my death." Everyone in the family should know where it is located, and upon that person's death, the file should be gone through *immediately* by the survivor.

Here's the kind of information that might be included:

Location of will
Name and address of attorney
List of checking and savings accounts and insurance policies
List of securities owned and their location
Location of safe-deposit box, key attached
Name of preferred funeral home and type of funeral preferred
If organs of the deceased are to be willed, note to that effect. (If organs are to be donated under the Uniform Anatomical Gift Act, at death the proper medical authority must be notified at once, since time is of the essence.)
Information on burial plot
List of honorary pallbearers
Location of all silver, jewelry, and other precious items
List of items that are to be willed to special people

The husband of my best friend is close to death. I want to be of help to her when it finally happens. I've never been through this before, so I'm at a loss to know just what I can do to help her. She will have plenty of emotional support from others; I want to be useful, because that will be the vacuum when the time comes.

When death comes, ask if you can coordinate arrangements for her, and then step right in. Call her lawyer, call the funeral home, and notify the cemetery in which her husband will be buried. Station someone by the telephone to answer all incoming calls. Give another friend a list to make telephone calls to the family's relatives and best friends scattered around, both locally and in other cities, to inform them of the sad news and of the funeral arrangements.

Call the newspapers to arrange for the insertion of the death notice. Help the widow carry out the exact wishes of the deceased about his funeral, according to the lawyer's instructions—wishes that were contained in his will.

If there are people coming from other towns for the funeral, arrange to have them met at the airport or train or bus station. Make sure they are lodged with other friends or at hotels or motels.

Have someone write in a book a meticulous list of all the telegrams, flowers, cards, and notes that arrive for the widow, so that in time she will be able to acknowledge them.

Help coordinate the wake, if there is to be one in the mortuary chapel or at home. Organize a luncheon for everyone in the family (including out-of-town friends) after the funeral service.

How is a newspaper death notice composed and placed?

This is something that should be done immediately, as soon as the funeral place, date, and time are known. One calls the death-notices section of the classified ads of both the morning and evening papers in the city (and suburban papers, too, if the deceased lived in a suburb).

Be sure that the information has been checked and rechecked, because it will all be done over the telephone (the paper will then bill the family of the deceased). Usually the paper will call back to recheck the facts and legitimacy of the call. (Yes, people *do* play miserable pranks like placing false death notices in the paper!)

The form for either a man or a woman is roughly as follows:

"Caldwell—James Karl, on January 14, 1982, beloved husband of Mary Louise Johnson Caldwell (the wife's maiden name is always listed, to help identify her) and father of Barbara, Joan, and Peter (the daughters' names are always given first). Funeral at St. Thomas More, 89th and Madison Avenue, at 11 A.M. Wednesday, January 17. Interment private." (If interment is not private, give name and address of cemetery.)

A person's age is given only if it's a child. One may put "suddenly" or "after a long illness" as an insert before the date of death.

Should a prominent person have his or her own obituary on file? Sounds very ghoulish to me, but I've heard it's important.

One of the great unanswered questions in life is when we're going to die. A prominent person owes it to his or her family, business, educational and philanthropic institutions to have a complete, accurate, up-to-date biography on file.

The information contained in this biography should be sent, along with the date of death and the list of survivors, to the city and suburban newspapers (these should be delivered by messengers), and to his or her college and boarding-school alumni magazines, professional-association magazines, and newsletters, clubs, etc.

A newspaper will call back to check for details, if the editor considers the obituary newsworthy. Even if one thinks the paper will certainly publish a lengthy obituary (which includes the funeral plans), it is better to arrange for the paid death notice anyway.

Should the divorced spouse of the deceased attend the funeral, even if there was great bitterness between them?

It certainly would be a nice gesture to attend the funeral. The former spouse would not sit up front with the family, however. He or she would join the other mourners behind the family.

How should one dress for a funeral? I have no black clothes for my good friend's services, and will probably feel very wrong.

You do not have to wear black anymore. Wear something conservative. A man wears as dark and as conservative a suit as he owns, with a quiet tie.

A woman should dress for a funeral in a non-décolleté, simple dress and shoes. Some women follow the old custom of wearing a hat in church, but it isn't necessary.

The widow should wear a black dress or suit for the occasion, borrowed if need be; if that is not possible, she should wear a somber, covered-up costume.

One sees the heavy black veil on the widow mostly at funerals in the "old country" today, or on the wife of a deceased head of state.

What are some of the nice things one can do for a friend when a death occurs in the family?

A really close friend can assume the role of the funeral coordinator or can take over the kitchen. When someone dies, there is a tremendous flow of people coming and going in the home, and the family has to be fed. (Among Jews, the supplying of food to the family at this time is a great tradition.)

Another way to help is to care for any small children who are underfoot, who need attention, and who don't really understand what has happened. Any grieving parent should appreciate the offer from someone to take the very young child out of the home during the prefuneral days, to keep them busy and amused.

What should I put on my card when I send flowers to a funeral? Just my name? Or a real message to the family, or what?

The message on a plain white card does not have to be any longer than this: "Deepest sympathy from John Williams."

You may also write just your name on the card, with no message at all. *Don't* send one of your business cards, however.

I'm confused about where one is supposed to send flowers—to the funeral home or to the church or to the cemetery.

One never sends flowers to an orthodox Jewish funeral, and often not to a conservative or reform funeral either. In Episcopalian funerals, flowers from the family and friends are permitted in church, but in a Catholic church, only the family's are allowed.

Often it's better to send flowers to the funeral home, where calls are received by the family. These flowers are later taken to the cemetery. If you send them, be sure to list your name and address on the back of the florist's card, to help in keeping accurate records, so that an eventual acknowledgment of your thoughtfulness can be made.

What is the custom of Catholic mass cards?

The Catholic or non-Catholic friend of a deceased Catholic often arranges with a priest for a mass or a group of masses to be said "for the soul of" the deceased. Sometimes the deceased's name is included in a novena of prayer by monks in a monastery or by nuns in a convent. Cards describing these actions are either mailed to the deceased's family by a church official or brought by friends calling at the funeral home and left on a tray provided for that purpose.

If you're very close to the family of the deceased, where do you make your call—at the house or at the funeral home?

Both. At the family home you should ask if there's any service you can perform to help. At the funeral home you would talk to the family for a while and sign the register. The signing should be a formal "Mr. and Mrs. Richard Pallavacini," not "Betty and Dick."

Does the family have to write a letter of acknowledgment to every single person who calls at the funeral home?

No—only if someone called at the funeral home and no one from the family was present at that particular moment.

Do all flowers sent to the funeral, and mass cards and statements of donations made to a fund in honor of the deceased, have to be acknowledged with a note?

Yes, by hand. If the person who dies was famous (a distinguished citizen of the community), a printed card of acknowledgment is all that is necessary, because there might be several hundred thoughtful acts to acknowledge. A message like this is sent on an engraved card with matching envelope.

> The family of Alice Grayson Mitchell
> gratefully acknowledges your most kind
> expression of sympathy

For close friends and distant relatives, a handwritten note is the nice way to say thanks. Split the task between members of the immediate family. Give each person a group of names to whom acknowledgments should be written. The note may be *very* short, like this:

Dear Mrs. Smith,

We were very touched by the beautiful flowers and your wonderful letter, so full of love and memories.

Mother had a great and full life. Your friendship meant a great deal to her. Thank you from all of us.

> Sincerely,
> Jeannie Drewes

Is it all right for me to end a donation to my own charity and then to notify the family that it was made "in honor of the deceased"?

It certainly is all right, but it's even better if the charity to which you give a donation concerns an organization or an activity with which the deceased was somehow associated.

If the family has not named any specific charity, you might remember a nonprofit cause for which the deceased was an active volunteer—like his or her church, college alumni fund, youth organization, etc.

Is it pushy if the family states in the death notice and in answer to the telephone queries, "Contributions may be made to the American Cancer Society" or to something like that?

It is not pushy, as long as the information is given on the telephone or in person *only* if asked. No one *has* to contribute. If you *do* contribute, make sure that the organization sends a card to the family of the deceased, informing them of your gift. The amount of money should not be stated.

If a woman's husband has died within the last few weeks, do you still send her a Christmas card, invite her to Christmas parties, and include her in celebration events, or is that considered to be bad taste?

Treat her as you would normally, but make a note of the sadness in her life. You can always write on the back of the cheerful Christmas card something like, "We are thinking of you every second, because this will be such a tough, hard Christmas. Next one will be better and the one after that much better. We love you."

Invite a relative of the recently deceased to any gathering you might have, like an open house or a dinner party or a picnic. If he or she does not feel like going out yet, your invitation will be declined, but certainly appreciated.

The nicest thing you can do for a widow or widower is to telephone and say, "Hey, how about coming over for a family dinner tomorrow night? We miss you."

The worst thing that you can do to a friend who has just lost someone is to consider that you did your part during the funeral and therefore you can forget that person for a few months.

Entertaining

Introduction

One of the greatest pleasures in life, as well as one of its most creative exercises, is the art of entertaining.

It *is* an art. It requires discipline, meticulous planning, and a continuous flow of new ideas and concepts. Unlike the creation of an artistic work, however, entertaining—to be truly successful—must be imbued with a large measure of unselfishness.

A good host is a kind person—one who really cares about the comfort and enjoyment of the guests. A good host is one who notices—and corrects—whatever is wrong. It may be someone who has no one to talk to; or that dinner is taking too long to be served; or that more wine is needed; or that the music is too loud; or that the room is too crowded and the guests should start to use another room.

In other words, a good host is someone who's *aware*.

You can hire the most expensive caterer in the world and still give the most expensive flop in the world, if you are unaware that guests are uncomfortable, that the atmosphere is strained, or that the timing is off. A good host takes action.

What's the first thing to do in planning a party? Is there any set plan to follow in organizing it?

I think there should definitely be a "Plan Sheet" for every party, with major headings and subheadings. Here's a typical list of *some* of the organizational topics to be addressed:

Party Plan

The reason for the party

(Example of reasons: Because we owe so many people; we wish to honor someone; it's a special anniversary; we want to start off the fund drive with a bang; we need to impress the business community.)

Whom are we going to invite?

Make up a guest list with a good balance of people.

What kind of invitation will we send?

Formal or clever.

What's the best date to give it?

Who will be the serving help?

(One's own children; a caterer; local college bartenders.)

What will the menu be?

What kind of wines and liquors will be served?

What will the table decor be?

(This section includes flowers that need to be ordered for the rest of the house.)

If it's to be a seated meal, what will the seating plan be?

(Place cards to be ordered?)

Entertainment: During cocktails? Dinner? After dinner?

Does parking for the guests require special planning?

Do the household pets need to be sent to a neighbor's house?

Do the small children need to go to "Grandma's house"?

Is the cleaning of slip-covers in the house a necessity?

Invitations

In giving an informal party, what kind of invitations are correct, and how far ahead of the date should they be sent?

Informal invitations may be handwritten on "informals" (good folded notepaper). Or they may be telephoned. Or they may be sent in a Mailgram if you have to reach a lot of people quickly. Or you may have them designed yourself and made up by a local printer. Or you may buy the "fill-in" kind of invitations found at your local stationer's or card store.

Informal invitations should be mailed three to four weeks before the party in a large city, and two to three weeks beforehand in a small community. People are so involved in so many activities today, they need enough time to rearrange their commitments around a party, which might involve anything from locating a hard-to-find baby-sitter to changing the departure date of a business trip.

If I have houseguests, may I bring them to a cocktail party to which I have been invited? What if it's a buffet supper, or even a seated dinner—can I suggest to my hosts that I'd like to bring them?

If you're invited to a cocktail party, call your host and ask if you could possibly bring them along. If your host has any hesitation in his or her voice before saying, "Of course, bring them," then realize your host is on the spot. There simply may not be enough room, and no one enjoys a cattle-market cocktail party. Be sensitive about that note of hesitation and answer, "It really might be better if we missed this one. We have a very busy schedule anyway while they're here, so give me a rain check, please, and have a beautiful party!"

Never try to bring a load of guests to a buffet supper, unless it's a resort community where everyone will be eating outside, and you know your hosts have the room and the money to enlarge their party continuously with other people's houseguests.

As a single woman I am always in a quandary about whether or not to bring a date when I'm invited to a party. Is there some sort of rule that governs this?

You should not bring a date unless it's a cocktail party or unless you call your hosts and ask if "it would help if I bring a date." Sometimes one's host doesn't know enough single men or women to invite and would appreciate a guest bringing a date. A host should put on the invitation something to communicate that fact, such as: "... cordially invites Ms. Mary Smith and guest."

If you are asked to bring a date and don't know anyone who would be suitable or enjoyable for you, tell your hosts you wish to come alone.

Remember, however, never arrive anywhere with an uninvited date without having previously talked to your hosts about it.

In this day of women's independence and equality, does a host still have to worry about his woman guest's getting home safely?

In many parts of the country, yes. If she does not have a car and if she has to return home alone, her hosts should see to it that one of the guests takes her home, or that a taxi is called, or that they drive her home themselves. All of this should be decided beforehand on the telephone.

If she has to travel by subway or bus late at night in a city like New York, it is unsafe. Other arrangements should be made.

I'm living with someone now, and my boss's wife has just asked me to a dinner party to serve, as she puts it, "as a much-needed single man." What should I do?

The only thing to do is to tell your boss's wife the truth. There is no way you can lie your way out of it. Call her and explain that you're terribly sorry, you will have to regret her very nice invitation, because you have a special relationship with a young woman now, and you are not free to accept.

Your hostess will then probably become embarrassed and feel she has to ask the young woman to dinner, too, although she doesn't have the room. So you should quickly step in, to save her from that predicament. Just say something like, "I hope you can meet her one day. I'll bring her over for a drink someday, when you're not having a big dinner, or you might come have a drink with us."

Then, if you really want to make a hit with the boss's wife, solve her problem for her. "You know, I have a good suggestion for an extra man, which is something you still need right now. How about Charlie Allen, who's also with the company? He's recently divorced, and I imagine he would very much enjoy coming to your house."

We have a group of prominent women coming from London to spend twenty-four hours with our company. We want to provide dinner partners for them at a kind of wrap-up business dinner. Do we dare suggest to the men in the company that they come without their wives or girlfriends to this event? The women officers in our company are also expected to attend without their spouses.

Absolutely. It's correct and proper to have a business dinner of that nature and communicate by memo that "because of limitations of space and the nature of the discussions, spouses are not invited."

If you're invited for dinner at seven o'clock, what is the right time to arrive?

Seven o'clock is obviously all right. (Not a minute before, however.) Anything up to seven-thirty is all right. Later than that begins to be rude. Arriving an hour late for dinner is just frankly impolite. If you are unavoidably detained, call your hosts, explain your reasons, and urge them "to go ahead and serve dinner right on time ... I will not need a cocktail. I do not wish to hold up dinner under any circumstances."

How long is a host supposed to wait dinner on a guest, and how long if it's the guest of honor?

The dinner must not be spoiled because of any tardy guest or group of guests. The hosts should begin their dinner punctually, even if it's the guest of honor who's late.

One does not punish the majority because of an action of the few.

Any guest who's unavoidably detained (inside a circling aircraft, for example, trying to land), would feel much more relieved knowing that the dinner party was progressing without him or her.

My parents taught me that, as a man, one of my social responsibilities was to seat the lady on my right at the table. Nowadays when I do it the woman always looks at me as if I had rocks in my head.

You were brought up correctly, in a traditional household. However, young women of today prefer to seat themselves at table and open their own car doors and do many things that run counter to the traditional roles of how a man is supposed to treat a woman and how a woman is supposed to expect him to treat her. This independence is a necessary part of women's being treated equally.

It *is* a new world. Don't feel rebuffed by the young woman who looks strangely at you. (She is being rude—she should smile and say thank you, instead of looking surprised.) But today's woman is able to take care of herself, and to ask for help when she can't. Men are learning to expect the same treatment from women—when a man is in any difficulty and a woman can help, then she should help and he should welcome it, too.

Just what makes a "guest of honor"?

When you seat people around your table, whether it's someone who comes to join your family Sunday lunch or whether you're giving a party in your home, the guest of honor is any of the following:

Your clergyman and spouse
Someone from a foreign country
Your visiting mother- or father-in-law
Someone with a birthday that day
Someone in public office (mayor, congressman, etc.)
A person who held public office in the past
An older person
Your houseguest
Your teacher or professor
Your boss

What are reminder cards, and how are they used?

Reminder cards help all of us who are absentminded and forgetful, with the proper information on the party. They are just like invitations, except there is no RSVP. The recipient of a reminder card has already accepted the party, and the card is sent for reference only.

How many of you have accepted a party by telephone and neglected to take down an important detail of the invitation, or else noted it inaccurately? A reminder card is something to stick in your bureau mirror or in your handbag or briefcase—all the infomation is there to refer to on party day.

Any host who has extended an invitation to a big party on the telephone or by "running into someone" by chance would be wise to send a reminder card to every guest who has accepted.

Here's a sample fill-in reminder card, available at stationer's. This may also be written by hand on your good notepaper:

This is to remind you that
Letitia Baldrige
expects you for *lunch*
on *Sunday, April 5th*
at *1* o'clock
1413 Sprague Street #3A

Here's a sample very informal handwritten reminder sent on one's notepaper:

The Mac Quades
wish to remind you that
you're expected for lunch
on Sunday, April 5
at 1 o'clock
1413 Sprague St., #3A

Seating a Table Properly

When do you use place cards? Does it have to be a fancy affair?

Use place cards whenever a party is eight or more. They help in seating. They are functional. Even for the most informal kind of party, guests are more comfortable and graceful when they know where they're supposed to go.

What form do you follow in making a place card?

You should put the guest's title and last name, such as:

Mr. Smith
Miss (or Ms.) Williams
Dr. Carter
Judge Eaton

If you have two Mr. Smiths, then you would put:

Mr. Robert Smith
Mr. William Smith

If you're having an informal party where everyone knows everyone, you can just write:

Bob
Sandra
Bill

Be sure to write the names *large*, so they can be read easily.

How do you get place cards?

You can buy them at a stationer's. For an informal party, you can make your own, cut out of your own stationery, or, if you are tying the cards in to your table decorating scheme, out of any paper or material that is used in the decorations. The place card may be a flat one or a folded "tent" kind.

If your handwriting is bad, can you type the place cards?

Absolutely. If no one can read your handwriting, the typewriter is for you. Use all capital letters, so the card will be easier to read.

Where do you put the place card on the table?

Anywhere above the place setting—over the top of the plate, leaning against the stem of the water glass, or resting on top of the dinner napkin.

What's the rule of seating people at a dinner party?

The male guest of honor sits on the hostess's right, the next-most-important man sits on her left. The female guest of honor sits on the host's right, and the second-most-important woman on his left, and so on.

Husbands and wives should not be seated together. In fact, if you are giving a party with several round tables of eight or ten, you should seat them at different tables.

Since guests are supposed to be seated man-woman, man-woman, what do you do when the host and hostess want to sit opposite each other at a table for eight?

A table of eight poses a seating problem. It can be solved in one of two ways:

In the first way, two men *do* have to sit next to each other, and two women *do* have to sit next to each other, but at least the host and hostess sit opposite each other.

	Woman	Woman	Man Guest of Honor	
Host				Hostess
	Woman Guest of Honor	Man	Man	

In the second way the host sits on the side, in order to keep the man-woman, man-woman ratio intact:

	Host	Woman	Guest of Honor Man	
Woman Guest of Honor				Hostess
	Man	Woman	Man	

If there's supposed to be an even number of each sex at a seated meal, what can one do when it seems all one's friends

*are widows and divorcées? I feel terrible putting two women
next to each other, and spend hours on the telephone trying
to round up single men.*

Don't spend your time on the telephone, particularly since
the results might not be fortunate. A woman would much
rather sit next to another attractive, intelligent woman than
be forced to make conversation with an unattractive dullard.

If you can match the sexes evenly, fine, but if you can't,
do not be upset. Women can sit very happily next to each
other, if the only extra men available are less than passable.

The same holds true when there are too many men and
there are no attractive extra women available. Two men
can enjoy sitting next to each other, too! (Unfortunately, the
older the generations grow, the fewer times a shortage of
women occurs!)

*At the last moment the other evening, a college friend of
mine arrived with her seven-year-old son and joined my dinner party. I didn't know where to seat him, so put him next
to me. Where should I have put him? My seating idea didn't
work well.*

A child, according to his or her level of sophistication,
would prefer to skip the dinner party (if he or she is twelve or
under). You should have given the little boy a tray upstairs in
front of the TV set. He would have been happier.

However, when something like that happens, you should
always place a small child next to his mother or father, who
can then bear the responsibility of seeing that he is amused
and eats properly.

The Service of Food at Parties

*Can our preteen child help out with our parties? Does it look
all right to the guests?*

A youngster can indeed help with your parties, and in
doing so, he or she will learn the basic factors of being a good
host.

Your child, for example, can be taught to take the guests'

wraps and hang them up nicely. He or she can be taught to pass hors d'oeuvres, to pass ice to those who need more, and to relay drink orders to whoever is tending bar.

When your guests go in to dinner, your child can collect all the empty glasses on a tray, put them in the dishwasher, wash out the dirty ashtrays, and put them back. Then there's the room where the guests had cocktails to be aired out, the cushions to be plumped up, and the room to be straightened up nicely, so it will be an inviting place to return to after dinner.

Your young child should not be serving your dinner guests at table, however, at the usual late dinner hour, because the guests might feel uncomfortable that he or she is not studying or in bed asleep.

We can't afford caterers, but with two teenage children in our family, there's no reason we can't have excellent "serving help" in the form of our children. They would like to learn how to do it the right way without our prompting, because once trained, they can earn good money this way—doing other people's dinner parties. How should they be trained?

Serving parties *is* an excellent way for young people to earn extra money. Here's a short primer for one person acting as a waiter or waitress for a dinner or luncheon with up to eight guests:

The First Course. The easiest way to serve the first course is, of course, to have it already in place on the table on "place plates" when the guests arrive at table. (A place plate is large, approximately twelve inches in diameter; it is used for decoration and to hold smaller plates and bowls, and it is usually removed permanently from the table at the end of the first course.) If, however, the host wishes the waiter to serve the first course to the guests, the waiter should bring in the plates of food (or soup plates) one at a time from the kitchen, holding it in his left hand and then placing it on each guest's place plate. (If there are no such things as "place plates" in the house, a dinner plate will do.) If it's desirable to speed up the service, the waiter would bring in a plate in each hand, one for a guest on his right, and one for a guest on his left. Unless the waiter is using both hands to carry two soup plates at a time, he carries one plate and serves a guest from the guest's left; he always removes a guest's plate, when he is finished eating, from the guest's right. The waiter should serve the woman guest sitting on the host's right, and then continue around the table counterclockwise. If a woman is hosting the dinner, then the first to be served would be the man on her right, and so on around the table. In each case the man or woman host is served last. (In Europe the hostess is often served first, and she begins eating immediately—a custom stemming from the medieval tradition of the royal host eating the food first, to prove to his guests that it has not been poisoned.) Before the next course is served, of course, the waiter removes the place plate and the soiled dishes from the first course. The waiter removes the plates from the right of each guest, or if the service needs to be speeded up, he removes from the left and the right simultaneously.

The Main Course. If the host is going to carve a roast at the table, the waiter brings it in on a warm platter balanced on his left hand (and steadied with his right). He would place it in front of the carver, and as the latter slices and places meat on each plate, the waiter takes each plate with his left hand and deposits it in front of the guest of honor, and so on around the table. It's easier for everyone, of course, if the meat is carved in the kitchen and arranged nicely on a garnished platter. The waiter would present this platter to each guest, balanced on a clean folded napkin on his left hand (to protect his hand from too much heat). The waiter should encourage each guest to take a serving of vegetable or garniture (like watercress) around the roast meat, fish, or fowl. If, after using the serving fork and spoon, the guest replaces them in a clumsy manner on the platter, the waiter should rearrange them nicely for the next guest's convenience. If the guest should drop the handle of the spoon in the sauce, the waiter should wipe off the handle with his napkin before letting the next guest use it. (The waiter would be smart to keep a napkin narrowly folded over his forearm for this reason.) The menu might offer two different vegetables to be served next, so the waiter would carry a bowl in each hand, again with his hands protected by folded napkins, if what he is carrying is very hot. He would offer the bowl in his left hand first, and then offer the right-hand bowl to the same guest next. If there is a gravy or a sauce for anything being served, it should be placed on a small tray and passed either in tandem with the main dish or directly following it.

The waiter should remember always to pass a platter or

bowl at a level comfortable to the guest—never too high and never so far back that the guest has to twist around to get at the food being passed. A good server remembers to keep the hot platters hot before serving them, and the cold platters cold. Caring about those little details makes the difference between a passable and a great waiter. A polished waiter often keeps his right hand behind his back while passing something in his left hand.

Rolls and Bread. The rolls, breadsticks, and other breads are passed separately by the waiter. The waiter might pass them during the first course, and again during the main course. The guest should put his bread on a bread plate, if there is one. Otherwise, the guest puts it on the plate for that course. In Europe, a guest often places the roll, breadsticks, or any kind of bread on the tablecloth next to the left part of his table setting. If there is no butter plate and you are eating a roll with the first course and have put it on your shrimp-cocktail underplate, and if it is about to be removed for the main course, you may take that remnant of roll and put it on the tablecloth or place mat to finish with the next course.

Subsequent Courses. If there's a salad-and-cheese course, the waiter would, of course, first remove the main-course plates and would then place an empty salad plate at each place. He would pass first the salad bowl, then the cheese tray, and finally a plate of crackers or breads.

Pre-Dessert. The waiter removes all the condiments and sauces that might be on the table. He also "crumbs the table," which consists of going to the left of each guest to brush crumbs onto a small tray or a clean plate or into a "silent butler."

Dessert. The host may have already placed the dessert fork and spoon on the table, as part of the original place setting—lying horizontally above the top rim of the plate. If he does not choose to set his table that way, the waiter must bring in the dessert utensils for each guest with the dessert plate. They are balanced vertically on the sides of the plate. The dessert may be served on the plates in the kitchen, or it may be served at table to each guest. If there is a sauce to be passed, the waiter would first offer the dessert with his left hand and then offer the sauce on a small tray with his right hand. There might be a fork and spoon as well as a doily with a bowl of water on top of it on the dessert plate. This is a finger bowl, and the guest is supposed to put the finger bowl on top of the doily to the upper left of the plate's position on the table, and put the dessert fork and spoon to the respective right and left of the dessert plate. The guest is now ready to receive dessert on the plate when the waiter passes it. If the bowl does not contain water, then the bowl should be left right on the plate. The dessert is meant to be spooned into it when it is passed by the waiter.

Coffee Service. Coffee is more elegantly served at the end of the meal, in demitasses arranged prettily on a tray, with their small coffee spoons lying symmetrically on the side of the saucer. The hosts may wish to have their coffee served at table, or they may wish to take it into another room and serve it there. This gives the guests a chance to stretch their legs and to mingle with other guests (a blessing if they have not liked their dinner partners!). On another tray there should be a pot of coffee, and another of decaffeinated brew. There should be a small jug of milk or cream, a bowl of sugar, and another of sugar substitute. The waiter can help keep the coffee brew hot by filling the pots with scalding hot water ten minutes before coffee is to be served. When the water is emptied and replaced by coffee in the pots, the temperature will remain hotter longer. If liqueurs are to be served, the waiter should bring to the coffee area a tray with tiny liqueur glasses, larger snifters for brandy, and the different bottles of liqueur. Either the waiter or the host asks each guest what he or she would like. It's a good idea for the waiter to pass at the very same time another tray full of tall glasses packed with ice and filled with water or club soda.

Manners at Table

When you're at someone's house for dinner and you're standing around the table, who sits down first?

Wait until the hostess sits. If she's busy bringing in things from the kitchen, she'll motion the guests to sit down without her, or else the host will tell everyone to be seated.

If you're at a large buffet party and people are taking a long time to be served and seated, you don't have to remain standing at your little table. Sit down—and you may also begin eating, while the food is hot. If your hostess should suddenly arrive to sit at your particular table, the men should either rise or make a motion of rising out of courtesy. Usually the hostess will take her seat so quickly the men won't have the time to get up to help her.

When do you begin eating at a large seated dinner?

Usually, when you are served. At a large dinner party, the hosts want their food enjoyed at its best moment—when it is piping hot. Usually the hostess will urge the people on her right, who have already been served, to start eating at once.

A young person should not begin eating until the adults around him do. In many families, there's often a rule that no one begins to eat until the parents are served and begin to eat themselves. This is good training.

Should a clergyman who's a guest in one's home be asked to bless the food before anyone eats, or does that embarrass him?

Invite the clergyman to bless the food as you approach the table. Everyone should remain standing until the blessing is finished.

The Food You Choose

I'm always perplexed about what menu to serve my guests. Either I give them too much food or too little. Are there any ground rules for structuring a menu for a party?

Balance is the one ground rule for any menu—a nutritional and a taste balance. One has to guard against a meal of all cream sauces, or one that is all fried. It is better to exaggerate in serving too light a meal than too heavy a meal.

A menu should depend on these basic factors:

1. Your budget.
2. Your time limitations—and the amount of staff you have or don't have to help you.
3. The time of day in which the meal is served (lunch should be lighter than dinner; a late supper should be lighter than dinner).
4. The foods that are fresh in season.

Here are some simple but tasty menus for a host who is very busy, who is the cook, and who has no help:

Lunch
Melon and prosciutto (Italian ham), cut into slices and decoratively arranged on each guest's plate
Quiche (served hot)
Mixed green salad (with tomatoes, scallions)
Lemon sherbet and homemade cookies
(White wine, well-chilled, served throughout, or if it's a very hot day, iced tea)

Everything can be prepared ahead. The host can spend all day at the office and serve his or her guests with ease the next day. The quiche can be made in advance and frozen. The salad greens can be washed, dried, and refrigerated the day before; the salad dressing made, the sherbet made, the cookies baked; the melon and prosciutto sliced and stored, well-covered.

Dinner
Vichyssoise, or any soup of which you are proud
Escalopes de veau sautés with lemon (or fresh fish filets)
Creamed spinach
Green salad
Hot buttered rolls
Chocolate mousse (or a wonderful fresh-fruit compote)
Demitasse
(White wine served throughout)

If you're saving on your effort and everyone's calories, you may forget the soup course.
The creamed spinach is frozen and only needs heating;

the mixed salad has been prepared the night before and the dressing is ready; the rolls have been purchased or made the night before, slit, buttered, and placed in the pan in which they will be heated, securely covered; the chocolate mousse is made the night before and refrigerated (a fresh-fruit compote is better made the night of the party); the veal scallops have been purchased and pounded paper-thin. The only work left is for the host to sauté them for a few minutes in a frying pan in butter (after dipping them in a highly seasoned flour), then adding lemon juice, consommé, herbs, and perhaps some white wine or dry vermouth to the sauce.

A Late Supper
A garnished platter with slices of cold turkey or chicken and rare roast beef
A salad of raw spinach leaves, mushrooms, and bacon with a vinegar-and-oil dressing
Hot buttered English muffins
A platter of different cheeses and some crackers
Bowls filled with fresh strawberries (cream and brown sugar on the side)

If you're going somewhere in a group, such as to a performance or an evening game, it's nice to have everyone come back afterward. Everything should be prepared in advance, so the hosts simply have to turn on the coffee percolator and put the food on the table.

According to what your friends drink, you would have an assortment of wine, beer, and liquor (soft drinks, too, of course) to offer.

Do I have to serve hors d'oeuvres before a lunch or dinner party? I don't eat them myself, and I don't know how to make them.

Since you will be giving your guests a fine meal, you do not have to serve elaborate hors d'oeuvres beforehand. You want to be sure your guests' appetites are directed completely toward the meal you have made them.

However, if someone has missed the previous meal, he or

she would like something to munch on while imbibing alcohol. You can answer that need by having a bowl of nuts on hand, or a plate of crackers with cheese cut into cubes. Even healthier: a platter of cut-up raw vegetables. (You don't have to make a dip—a tiny dish of salt and one of pepper are sufficient.)

Guests on Diets

What do you do if you're on a strict weight-loss diet and you're invited to a dinner party? Can you eat beforehand?

It's kinder to your hosts if you do not accept the invitation. It's rude to sit there and eat nothing. People don't like to be around a heroic noneater who makes them feel guilty with every bite they take. The hosts who have labored over their food are affected by it. When you're on that kind of diet, it's the time to see your friends *between* meals.

A person who is just watching his weight can be careful, take very small portions of food, and even push some of it around on his plate, pretending to eat it. If he does that, and if he does not discuss his diet (the subject that is probably the most boring one in the entire world), he will be a polite and welcome guest.

What do you do if you have terrible fish allergies and can't eat fish at a dinner party?

Often you'll know in advance that fish will be the main part of the menu, because the hostess will say, "We're going to have Maine lobster," or the host will brag about his freshly caught fish to be broiled. If you know about the fish, that's the time for you to say, "You know, I can't eat fish, so will you please give me a rain check?"

If the fish is a surprise, don't eat it. Just push it around a bit on your plate, but say nothing.

The perfect host asks his guests during the cocktail hour, when fish is on the menu, "Is anyone here allergic to fish?" If the answer is yes, he replies something like, "We have chicken salad all prepared—for you."

Menu Cards

When do you use menu cards? Where do you get them?
What do you put on them? Where do you put them?

You can use menu cards for formal dinners in your home
or when you're entertaining in a public place. They are nice
as a souvenir of a special event, like a birthday, anniversary,
or special Christmas lunch. You can buy them at a stationer's
or you can make them yourself by cutting out a rectangular
shape (4½″ x 6½″, for example) out of heavy stock.

A menu card is placed to the left of a person's place at
table, next to his outside fork. Or it can be balanced against
the water glass, or it can be balanced on top of the napkin
when it is in the center of the plate.

Following is a menu card proudly made by some young
children in honor of their grandmother's birthday.

October 11, 1980

NANA'S 75TH BIRTHDAY DINNER

Seafood Cocktail (brought by Dougie)

Chicken Sauté Chasseur (made by Stephanie)
Baby Peas
Carrots Glacé (made by Mom)
Salad Mimosa (Jeanie's special)

Dad's Ice Cream
Birthday Cake (we all made it)
Coffee
(Nana shouldn't drink it)

Menu cards for a formal dinner are on white or ecru stock,
but menus for special-event parties may be of any color.
Black ink may be used (by someone with a good hand), or
they may be typed. If there are matching place cards, those
should be written by the same hand.

Here's a sample of a more formal menu, with the host's monogram:

F G H

April 1, 1982

Dinner

Eggs à la Russe

Filets of Sole Florentine
Grilled Tomatoes with Mushrooms
Endive Salad

Fresh Raspberries à la crème
Dentelle Cookies

Demitasse

Inglenook chablis
Pinot Chardonnay

The wines are listed (with their vintages if there are any, at the lower left, or on the left-hand margin across from the course during which it is served).

Service of Wine

Occasionally, hosts like to serve sherry with the first course (usually with something like a clear soup); the waiter would pour the very small sherry glasses almost full.

If both a white and a red wine are to be served, the white is served next, with the fish course, then the red wine (in the larger of the two wineglasses).

The red wine should be opened at least a half-hour before

dinner. It's uncorked in order to "breathe" and to become room temperature. It's a good idea to uncork the white wine at this time, too, then recork it and put it back in the refrigerator. (The white wine is opened ahead simply as a time-saver—it isn't supposed to "breathe.")

The host should instruct the waiter beforehand *when* he wishes him to start serving the wine; also, *how quickly* he wishes him to fill up the glasses. It's very hospitable to have the waiter keep the glasses filled from the minute one sits down to the minute one leaves the table, but there may be strong reasons for not doing this. Guests who have had too much to drink, for one example. Not having enough wine on hand is the more usual reason!

The waiter should fill the normal-size wineglass half full to two-thirds full. If the wineglass is an oversized "bucket" glass, he would fill only the bottom quarter of the glass.

In a private home the waiter does not go through the gesture of bringing the cork to the host to sniff or have the host take the first taste to make sure the wine is all right. (That has presumably already been taken care of in the kitchen by the host before the wine is brought to the table.)

When the waiter is finished pouring the wine into a glass, he slowly twists the bottle neck in one circular motion as he brings the bottle slowly upright. This stops the flow of the wine but also impedes the splashing of drops. (He may also have a napkin wrapped around the bottle to protect the table linen.)

If the host has a wine basket (which cradles the bottle in almost a horizontal position), it's a good thing for the waiter to use, because it assures that the sediment from the bottom of the bottle does not pour out with the wine.

If the party is informal, the host will place a coaster at either end of the table and have the waiter bring in a bottle of red and a bottle of white, or two bottles of either kind to keep on the table. The host would pour from his end, and perhaps pour each glass around the table. Then he would urge the guests to help themselves to more wine when desired. The waiter should keep careful watch on these bottles, and replenish them without the host's having to remind him.

If a guest touches the rim of his wineglass as the waiter approaches with the wine bottle, that is a signal to the waiter: "Please do not pour wine in this glass," or, "I've had enough; do not serve me any more."

If your guests completely finish their white wine, down to the last drop, isn't it all right to pour red wine into their same glasses?

No. Either have separate clean wineglasses on the table for the red or wash the dirty glasses and bring them back to the table.

We are not wine drinkers. If we're giving a party, what kind of wines should we stock in order to take care of our wine-drinking friends' pleasure—from cocktail hour through dinner?

For the cocktail hour you might have on hand dry or sweet sherry, or dry or sweet vermouth, or any of the popular "aperitifs." Many choose a glass of dry white wine at the cocktail hour (either chilled or "on the rocks").

For the first course, or to drink with any fish, salad, chicken, veal, or fruit, a chilled white wine is nice (such as a Chablis, Soave, Riesling, Chenin Blanc, Pinot Chardonnay).

For the meat or game course (or the salad with cheese), serve a Burgundy, Bordeaux, Chianti, Cabernet Sauvignon, or Zinfandel at a cool room temperature (from 60 to 70 degrees).

Rosé wines should be chilled, like white wines. A rosé is best served with a light dish and is more popular in hot weather than in cold.

For dessert you may serve the same wine you had from the previous course. Or if it's something festive like an anniversary, dessert time is the moment to bring on the champagne (the drier the better!).

Some people enjoy a sweet wine with dessert, such as port or a sweet sauterne or sherry, but one seldom sees this custom followed anymore in this country.

If you're giving a really formal dinner party, with a menu like turtle soup, a fish course, wild fowl, and a dessert, what wines do you serve and where do you put all the glasses?

That sounds like a royal feast. You'd place the small sherry glass to the far right, the white-wine goblet next to it (on the left), then the red-wine goblet, and to its left the water gob-

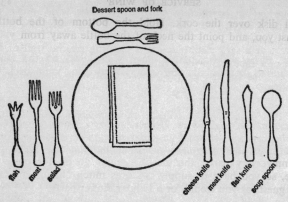

Dessert spoon and fork

fish meat salad   cheese knife meat knife fish knife soup spoon

let. Above these glasses, you might place the champagne glass for dessert.

It's easier for the server if you line up your glasses, more or less in a straight line, and the server can begin on the outside right and work inward, as each new wine is served during each new course.

Is it all right to put a half-gallon of wine on the table at a dinner party?

It's much more elegant to pour the oversized wine bottles into decanters, which you refill as needed.

I've heard that if you put wine in a decanter, that means it's not very good, and you don't want people to see the label.

That's not true except for hosts who are trying to fool their guests. Frankly, a good wine tastes good from the bottle or from the decanter. The guest knows it the minute he tastes it. A poor wine is not going to be upgraded by being served in a fancy cut-crystal bottle.

How do you open a bottle of champagne?

It's better to do it in the kitchen unless you're an experienced champagne-bottle opener. First untwist the little wire loop on the side of the cork; remove it. Then remove the metal disk over the cork. Hold the bottom of the bottle against you, and point the neck of the bottle away from you, pointing at a safe place (not at a painting on the wall or at someone's face). Slowly turn the cork and ease it up with your thumbs (or else give it a quick twist with your fingers).

How many people does a bottle of champagne serve at dessert time?

Normally four. If you're at a wedding-rehearsal dinner or an anniversary party, the toasting might go on for quite a while, so you have to supply twice as much champagne for your guests as you would for a regular dinner party.

If you receive a case of wine as a present, how is it best stored to use for a "very special occasion"?

Keep it in a cool dry place, such as a cellar where the temperature is from 55 to 65 degrees (ideally). Make sure that if the bottles are corked, they are laid on their sides (to keep the cork from drying out). A wine rack is very useful for this.

Bottles that are screw-capped may be stored in an upright position on a shelf where it's dark and cool.

What kind of glass is best to buy for wine?

There are white- and red-wine glasses, but today you may buy an "all-purpose" wineglass, such as a ten-ounce tulip-shaped stem goblet that is suitable for the serving of any wine, including champagne.

The glass should be thin, sparkling clear, with its rim smaller than the base of the bowl.

I've seen people holding the wineglasses to the light, twirling the wine around inside, and performing what look like mysterious ceremonies with wine. What's it all about?

Wine lovers will gaze with intense concentration at the color of the wine, holding the glass to the light. They hold white-wine glasses by their stems (so as not to remove the chill from the wine). They will often cup their red-wine glasses in the palm of their hand, to warm its contents, and they will swirl the wine around a bit to sniff its bouquet to the fullest. They will take a tiny sip, to test its taste on their taste buds.

The person who orders wine in a restaurant or club might be presented the cork by the sommelier (wine steward) or the captain. He sniffs it to assure it is not a dried-out cork (which might affect the quality of the wine). The wine steward or captain will next pour a small portion of wine into the host's glass, which the latter immediately tastes, and then nods approval to the Captain. All the others at the table are then served their glasses of wine, and the host's glass is filled at the end.

If a woman is hosting the group, the same routine is followed. If the wine has indeed turned to vinegar, the host should mention this quietly to the captain, who should then be offered a sip of the wine to find out his opinion. If the wine is bad, the bottle will be removed and another one brought.

It is the most gauche thing in the world for someone who does not know anything about wine to think it is impressive "to send back the wine." It should be done only when one is knowledgeable and certain of what he or she is doing.

I have a small room in our home that is cool and dry, so we are starting a "wine cellar" there. How should I organize it?

Keep a little notebook in your "cellar" in which you record the following information about each bottle of wine you purchase:

1. The name of the wine and the winery that made and bottled it.
2. The date each bottle was purchased.
3. The price.
4. How many bottles were purchased.
5. The date each one is removed and consumed.
6. Your own and your guests' opinion of that particular wine.

What are you supposed to do if the wine spills at your place? Ignore it? Mop it up? Let the host take care of it?

If wine spills on someone's good linen or on the table surface, whether it's your fault or not, action must be taken at once. Tell your host, get a dish towel and some club soda. Slide the towel under the wine stain and clean the spot from the table. Pour club soda on top of the red stain (not necessary if it's white wine or champagne) and let it sink in. If there's no club soda available, pat the wine stain as dry as you can, then rub a lot of salt into it with your fingers. This helps make the stain removable in the laundering of the linen.

If there's an ugly red stain in front of you, cover it with a clean napkin.

If the hosts soak their linen in cold water all night after the party, the stain will probably disappear with a subsequent laundering.

Toasting

If you are giving a small informal dinner at home, is it all right to make a toast? I have heard that toasting is for "grand occasions" only.

Toasting is one of the nicest customs there is of making an outside person feel at home at your table. Even the youngest child should learn to raise his mug of milk in a toast—a salute, really—to a person who has come to his house. It is appropriate at the most informal of gatherings to "raise a toast."

It seems Europeans usually toast their guests at the beginning of a meal, and the Americans at dessert time. Which is better?

Either is fine. It's nice of the hosts, at the beginning of the meal, to greet the guests with a short word of welcome. The host or hostess could rise, raise the wineglass, and say to the guests, "Welcome to our house. Your being here makes this a very special night for us." This is our version of the Scandinavian *"Skål,"* the French *"À votre santé,"* and the Italian *"Cin-cin."*

Then it's nice if one of the guests at dessert time lifts his

or her glass and says, "To our hostess—the cook. Thank you
for a perfectly beautiful dinner!"

*I love to make toasts, because I'm good at it, I guess. But
I'm a woman and I always feel intimidated if I make a toast
before anyone else has. It's as though I have taken someone
else's prerogative.*

No, you have not, unless you begin too early. Wait until
dessert time—toward the end. If no one has made a toast,
then it's obvious no one is going to.

The best toast for you to make if you want to get on
your feet at that point is to your hosts—thanking them for
a superb dinner (even if it's hamburgers—because a hamburger dinner may be very superior). It's a nice thing to do.
The other guests feel good, and your hosts certainly do.

The one time it's tricky to raise a toast when no one else
has is when you're the guest of someone and your host has
not raised a toast to the guest of honor.

If your host is an insecure sort of person, your raising a
toast when he should have might make him feel ill-at-ease.
You have to be the judge of whether your toast would delight
or intimidate your host.

*Is it better to make an extemporaneous toast or a well-re-
hearsed, written one?*

That depends on you. If you have rehearsed your toast over
and over, you have probably memorized it, and it's better not
to read it. If you have something like a complicated original
poem, that, of course, must be read, but everyone loves to
listen to a good, cheerful extemporaneous toast.

Oscar Wilde said of toasting, "Follow the Three B's. Begin,
Be Brief, and Be Seated."

Is it all right to give an off-color toast?

Well-intended dirty stories just never go over in mixed company the way you had hoped. There are always some people
in the group who feel awkward about it, and their discomfort ruins the others' good humor.

What Happens After Dinner

How soon after dinner is it polite for a guest to leave?

After coffee has been served, a guest may leave within half an hour; it helps if he or she has a nice excuse ready. Everyone should leave within an hour after coffee is served—unless there is dancing or entertainment, which changes the complexion of the party and turns it into a late-night affair for those who wish.

Even if there is dancing, a guest may take his leave within an hour of leaving the table.

As a hostess, I am often bothered by certain guests who refuse to leave. I have to get my sleep, because of a very demanding job. How does one gracefully get rid of guests who stay too long?

Don't bother being graceful about it. Just be good-humored. Stand up and say with a broad smile, "Well, some of us have to run the world tomorrow, so we have to get some sleep. The more important we are, the earlier we have to get to bed!"

Everyone will laugh and get the hint. If a guest persists, just get his or her coat and push the person gently toward the door with an "I know you need your sleep as much as I do." People who stay too late are bores *and* boors, and one must be firm with them.

What is the best thing of all to have happen after a dinner party? Clever games?

No, good conversation. Good conversation is the best thing that can happen to any breakfast, lunch, or dinner party. When your guests are relaxed and have had their coffee, split them up into small conversational groups. Make sure each group has a talkative person, a good conversation maker. He or she will draw the others into a favorite topic of conversation. People who have been immersed in each other during the entire dinner should definitely be broken up. The host can do it smilingly: "You have to go spread your charms around,

Charlie." ... "You've held him spellbound long enough, Alice. There are other people who want to be spellbound."

Flattery will get a host almost anywhere.

What about after-dinner music?

Good music after dinner is a marvelous continuation of the relaxed feeling a host wants his guests to have. A good pianist (not Cousin Louis); a surprise jazz harpist; good musical tapes that change the beat every so often and that are played at a volume that encourages, not discourages, conversation, the classical chamber-music quartet from the local university, the faculty jazz trio from the local high-school music department —there is always a wealth of talent available to be tapped at home or nearby.

If you ask soloists or classical groups to perform, make their programs short—from twenty to thirty minutes. People with full stomachs at the end of the evening are often not up to a long program, no matter how great the musicians are.

What about games?

Games are fine, but not after too big a meal and too long an evening. People who don't like games and would rather talk should have a small room into which they can flee without criticism during the games.

If you're going to have a game after your dinner party, call a couple of friends, explain how it works, and ask their help to get it going properly. Sometimes all it takes is some fired-up enthusiasm from just one quarter—other than the host's.

Is it all right to watch certain TV programs after dinner when one has guests? Programs they would enjoy too?

If your next-door neighbor or your brother-in-law drops in for dinner informally and you all want to see the same program after dinner, that's perfectly all right.

If you have a dinner party, the only excuse for watching television afterward is if the President of the United States is making an important address or some earth-shaking news story is breaking that everyone is concerned about.

An entertainment show on television is *not* a component of a successful dinner party. If the dinner party has to turn on "the tube," it's a sign of a complete breakdown of any interest in what anyone has to say about anything.

When you hire a band to play for dancing, how do you instruct them politely?

Well, first of all, discuss every single detail with a representative of the group long before your party. Have a distinct understanding of all costs you will incur, and what happens costwise if you want the band to play beyond the hour that's stipulated in the contract. Be sure they know what kinds of music you want, and that you know what must be done on your end to prepare for their appearance. Discuss acoustics, extension cords, and other electrical requirements. Discuss lighting of the area where you'll be dancing, the rental of a proper piano, and other important logistics.

When they arrive, be sure to show the musicians to a room where they can change their clothes and to a bathroom they can use. Arrange to have them given light refreshment during their "breaks," too.

Usually there's a three hour minimum. If you wish to go beyond the stipulated contract, the head of the band will come up to you about fifteen minutes before and ask if you want them to play another hour.

One does not tip the musicians. If they were particularly good, write them a letter of appreciation they can show to other potential prospects, which will help get them other jobs.

Problems of Alcoholism

If you have a friend who has become an alcoholic, how do you handle him at your party?

Don't invite him to a large cocktail party, where you can't control how often he or she goes to the bar. Invite your friend to come to lunch or dinner, about twenty minutes before you sit down to eat. Make the pre-meal drinks weak. Serve wine very sparingly during your meal.

The major worry in inviting an alcoholic friend or any heavy-drinking friend, for that matter, is being responsible for his or her leaving your home behind the wheel of an automobile, in no condition to drive.

If a guest is not fit to drive, be sure a taxi is called or that one of your other guests or you yourself drive that person home. Remove the keys from his pocket or her handbag if the person who has had too much to drink insists on driving.

If the person escapes from you behind the wheel of his or her car, call the police and report the fact. Far better to have the person apprehended by the law for driving under the influence of alcohol than to be responsible for letting the person kill himself or other innocent people.

Is there any possibility of a host contributing toward a friend's reliance on alcohol by having too long a cocktail hour before dinner?

Absolutely. All over America, hosts are adding to the statistical total of more than ten million alcoholics in the country by consistently keeping their cocktail hours twice as long as they should be. Forty-five minutes is long enough before any meal. Half an hour is better.

Are parents sometimes responsible for turning their children into alcoholics?

Alarmingly so. The children see their parents abuse alcohol at home and think it's the smart "adult" thing to do. They see their parents rush to the bar when they return home at night, seeking a quick "feel-good" relief from the bottle. They naturally want to have that "feel-good" sensation themselves.

The parent who drinks in moderation and who is always in control of himself is a great influence on his or her child. The guest who arrives out of control because of alcohol or any other mind-altering drug should be pointed out to the children as an example of the greatest human tragedy there is.

This is how children learn how to resist drug abuse themselves.

When a friend is a recovering alcoholic, how do I treat him when he comes to my home?

Exactly like any other guest. Make no comment. Ask him or her the same question you ask anyone: "What would you like to drink?"

The recovering alcoholic will request something like a soft drink (or coffee or tea or fruit juice). Make sure that whatever you serve that person is in a beautiful glass or handsome cup and saucer.

Put a wineglass at his or her place at the table. Do not turn his wineglass upside down. The recovering alcoholic will touch the rim of the glass in a gesture of "no thanks" when the wine is being passed.

Is a recovering alcoholic susceptible to liquor in cooking even when it is a very small amount?

Sometimes. In a dish where wine or brandy is added before the mixture comes to a boil, like a stew or casserole, the alcohol boils away and is no longer alcohol. But in desserts, where cognac or liqueur are added and not cooked, the dish is dangerous. Watch your menu carefully.

Working with a Caterer

We are going to have to give our first big party, and I will have to hire a caterer. Just what can I expect of this service?

A properly trained caterer and his or her staff will prepare all the food and serve it (properly attired), as well as provide the extra tables and chairs and all the equipment needed to handle the party logistics. They will set everything up, and clean it all up, leaving your home exactly as it was before they arrived.

How do you find the right caterer to do the job?

By word of mouth. A successful caterer has an established reputation in town, and just because a certain caterer "did" your best friend's party, that doesn't mean that if he does your party it will look the same. Each party is approached as an individual, unique affair.

Should you compare estimates from different caterers for your party?

Absolutely, yes, if you are watching the budget, do compare prices. Remember, however, that most caterers' prices are pretty much the same. It's the quality of the menu and the wines that make the prices skyrocket.

How far ahead should one book a caterer?

If you want one for the Christmas season, book him or her at least six months ahead. For a less busy time, book the caterer two months ahead.

If I'm having a big dinner party, should I have the caterer bring all the china, crystal, and flatware, or should I have him bring things to supplement what I have?

Some caterers prefer to bring everything, from the bar glasses to the after-dinner coffee cups. They don't like to have their staffs responsible for breaking "something precious" in the host's home.

If the hostess wants to use her own linens and items like special plates, the caterer will, of course, utilize her things.

Are gratuities included in the caterer's bill?

Usually they are not. Be sure you ask that question in advance. If you're tipping, remember to give about twenty dollars to the "party supervisor," ten dollars each to the head-waiter and head cook (or even fifteen dollars each, if you were specially pleased), and five dollars to everyone else on the staff.

How do caterers charge?

Some charge by the hour, with a four-hour minimum. Others charge a set fee for the entire job, with a cost per head for each guest.

The hosts should avoid overtime charges and dismiss the caterers at the hour when it was contracted they could leave.

If certain guests are having too good a time and staying on, a demi-bar can be set up in a central spot that the guests can operate themselves; then the caterers can go home.

What should a host guard against in dealing with the caterer?

Last-minute changes in the kind of food and wines to be served, staying in the area where the staff is working hard to set up—it throws them off schedule when the host keeps interrupting; allowing small children to play underfoot—it's impossible to be both efficient caterers and baby-sitters, too!

Table Settings

Is it all right to use the napkins from one set of linens and the tablecloth or place mats of another?

The most accomplished hosts do it all the time. You can mix and match linens to your flower centerpiece, to the colors of your draperies and chair seats, to the colors of the dining-area rug, or even to the theme of your party. If, for example, you have a pale blue cloth with matching napkins, and at Christmastime you want to use bright red napkins from another set, it's fine to do it—particularly if you have red candles or red in your centerpiece.

Is it all right to use food as a centerpiece—like a birthday cake, for example, or a salad?

It's a great idea, provided the centerpiece is consumed at the end of the meal and one won't have to stare at an empty space in the middle for too long.

I have a one-room apartment. I want very much to have six for dinner every so often. How is it possible to have a sit-down dinner in such a small space?

Keep a collapsible round card table in a closet. Find a carpenter who will make six very small inexpensive benches for you which you can make comfortable with soft cushions. Three of the benches could be used around your apartment normally, and three of them could be stacked and stored in your closet when you're not entertaining. Six people sitting on small benches can fit very well at a round card table.

How should napkins be folded for a lunch or dinner party?

There are many ways, so many, in fact, that there are books on the subject. At informal meals one may stick them like flowers into the wineglass; they may be folded like fans across the dinner plate.

The two classic ways are shown here:

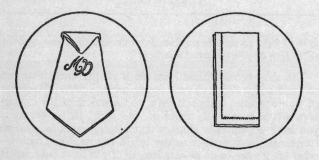

If there's a monogram, it should be prominently displayed.

I'm tired of using flowers in a bowl and silver candlesticks for every dinner party we have. What are some other possibilities?

Try putting that bowl of flowers on a sideboard with the silver candlesticks flanking it. You might try making a pattern of little votive candles on your table instead. Or use your outdoor hurricane lamps (their glass bells filled with daisies and strawberries). You might place anything you collect—porcelain figurines, pewter mugs, ivory objects, wooden animals —down the center of your table. Use pots of flowering geraniums, or put clusters of baby's tears plants in front of each guest's place. Take your coffee mugs, fill them with wildflowers, and put one at each place. Take your dessert bowls

and put one at each place, filled with water afloat with holly-
hock blossoms. Put one tulip in a bud vase and put it at each
place. Place a large bowl of bright red apples in the center,
and tuck little white flowers into the spaces between the apples. Place terra-cotta pots full of fresh herbs down the center,
interlaced with small white candles, and use fresh green and
white linens.

In other words, loosen up your imagination.

Can I use contrasting patterns in my table linens?

Certainly, as long as the color scheme is basically the same
between the two patterns.

*Why do some people set the table without any linens whatso-
ever except for napkins?*

Our ancestors in the seventeenth and earlier centuries ate
that way. They liked the bare wood surface. Today, many
people follow suit when they are proud to show off the beautiful wood surface of their antique tables or an unusual surface
of their modern tables. There's usually a small circle of straw,
felt, or some kind of fabric under each plate so that the heat
or cold of the plate will not hurt the table surface beneath.

Setting the Table Properly

How do you know where to place the flatware on the table?

It's very easy—and logical. Flatware is placed with its handles an inch from the bottom edge of the table. It is arranged
on both sides of the area where the plate goes. One uses one's
flatware from the outside in (from both left and right sides),
as each course progresses.

Let's say you're going to eat a many-course meal, beginning
with soup and going through a fish, meat, salad-and-cheese,
and soufflé dessert course. (Note how the sharp sides of the
knife blades are always turned into the plate.)

Where do you put a seafood fork in a place setting?

Either on the far right or on the far left, or on the under-plate of the seafood cocktail as it is brought in from the kitchen.

Do you have to use a butter plate?

They're being used less and less, partly because some people never serve bread, even at parties, and partly because it's all right to put an unbuttered piece of bread or roll on the table-cloth.

If you are serving something like hot biscuits or popovers, with which butter and jam or honey are served, butter plates should be used.

Where does the butter knife go on the butter plate?

Across the top of the plate, the blade toward the user.

When you're passed a relish tray with celery and olives, are you supposed to put them on the plate under your soup bowl or on the butter plate?

On the butter plate, if you have one, on the underplate if you don't.

Where do you put the soup spoon? In the soup bowl or on the plate?

Always rest a spoon not in use on the underplate or saucer of anything you're eating or sipping with it. That includes the spoon with which you eat your fruit cup, the spoon that stirs your coffee and tea, etc.

I know that the main plate is put in the middle of a place setting. But where are the butter and salad plates placed, and does the coffee always go on the right?

Yes, the coffee and tea cups and saucers are always placed to the far right of the flatware on the right.

The butter plate should be placed to the upper left of the place setting, and the salad plate to the bottom left.

A glass of iced tea or coffee goes on the upper right, above the knives, just as a wineglass would.

Is there a rule about how tall candles should be?

Above eye level, if possible, so the flame doesn't cause a glare in the guests' eyes.

May candles be lit on a luncheon table?

It doesn't look right. In fact, candles should not even be on a luncheon table.

Does it matter what color the candles are at a dinner party?

The candles may certainly be color-cued to the table setting, but remember one thing: white is *always* right.

Is it all right to use different china patterns with each separate course?

Absolutely. In fact, it's perfectly all right to mix patterns within a course.

Is it rude to pick up a plate at someone's dinner table and turn it over to examine its markings?

No, it's a compliment to one's hosts—as long as one exclaims, "What perfectly beautiful plates!" If you say nothing after examining them, it might be construed as a criticism.

The Formal Dinner Party

When is a dinner party truly a "formal" one?

When engraved invitations are used and guests are asked to come in formal evening dress (the words "Black Tie" are put on the lower-right-hand part of the invitation).

When a real chef is in the kitchen and a butler and his formally dressed waiters do the serving (one to every six guests).

When four or five courses are served, with three or four wines.

When there is a seating chart, called the *"plan de table,"* after the French, in which little white cards bearing the guests' names are inserted into a leather model of the table. The butler shows it to each guest as he or she arrives, so that the guest can see where he sits and between what two other people.

When only the finest linens are used, and sterling-silver, gold, or vermeil table services.

The Buffet Party

We want to have twenty for a buffet supper in our small apartment. How should we go about organizing it?

The first thing to think of is: will your apartment hold twenty people comfortably? If not, reduce your guest list and give perhaps two such parties instead of one.

There should be room for every single person to sit down comfortably and have some sort of base to rest a plate of food and a glass of wine upon (a table edge, a TV table, a bookshelf, a piano bench, etc.).

You might need to borrow a card table or two. If you clear some bookshelves, you may use those as serving areas.

Give your guests oversized napkins that they can spread on their laps to protect their clothes (because a buffet in a small area usually causes spills and stains). If you don't own any large napkins, buy some cotton remnants in marvelous patterns and make your own. They will always come in handy.

Keep your cocktail selection small. You will be too busy with other logistics to have to worry about a large menu of drinks. White wine, premade martinis, and Scotch or bourbon highballs ought to do it. (Always have cold beer on hand if you're in the younger generation, and plenty of soft drinks and club soda for those who don't want alcohol in any generation!)

Keep your cocktail hour short, then have someone pass with a tray collecting everyone's drinks and dirty ashtrays. Get everyone into line for the food, and while they're doing that, tell them where you would like them to sit (something you will have worked out ahead of time and have all written down). This is a smart thing to do, because your guests will be relieved knowing where to sit, and you can place them with whatever conversational partners you want them to have.

Be sure you have an easy menu. The best kind is something that does not even require a dinner knife—no meat cutting. Something like goulash, beef à la bourguignonne, chicken Tetrazzini, for example, served with rice or noodles. Prebutter the rolls, so you won't have to serve butter and give your guests butter knives. A big mixed salad and dessert should complete your menu. With a menu like the above, all your guests would need are a dinner plate and fork, and a dessert plate and spoon or fork. (Easy work for the cleanup detail, too.)

Have the wine bottles or decanters and empty glasses on a tray near the food area—also glasses filled with water for the non-wine-drinkers. The dessert service could be set up in yet another serving area, and the coffee service in still another.

Every inch of your apartment space should be utilized. Borrow large trays to help speed the logistics. Some people who entertain large groups in a small space use the second bathroom as the bar—by putting a large plank over the tub, which is then used as a table and an efficient working area. Ice is kept in a container in the tub, too.

The buffet hosts should have a person who spends the entire time collecting dirty plates and glasses, as well as replenishing the buffet. This "hired hand" may be a neighbor, a college student, a young relative. One's guests should not be trooping out into the kitchen, carrying their plates. A traffic jam and confusion would be the only result.

If you have a great deal of space in which to set up a buffet (a dining room, for example), make it look as pretty as possible. Each serving dish should be placed on a trivet to protect the table beneath, with the serving implements lying beside it. One nice flower arrangement in the center suffices on the buffet. For an evening party, put out as many candles as you have, to light the area. (Different candlesticks, votive candles, taper sticks, anything to hold a candle can be arranged attractively on the serving table.)

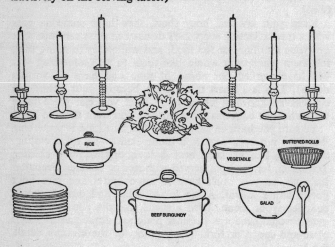

Do women have to be served first in a buffet line?

No, whoever congregates first in the buffet serving area goes ahead and serves himself. Usually a woman guest starts off the parade of people at the buffet. The hosts usually bring up the end of the line.

Is it the polite thing to do for a man to fetch a plate of food for his dinner partner at a buffet party?

No, unless she has an obvious handicap, such as sitting there with a large cast on her leg and crutches. People like to pick and choose their own food, in their own preferred amounts.

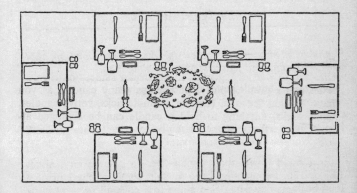

Let's say you want to have friends for dinner—a total of six people in your home. Is it better to have the dishes of food put down on the table and have everyone pass them around, or is it better to place the food on a side table and have them serve themselves buffet-style?

Buffet-style. If possible, use electric hot trays to keep your serving dishes warm, so that seconds can be served and the food remains hot.

When it comes time for a second helping, at a large party, each guest serves himself. At a small party, the host or hostess should take the plate of each guest and serve him some more of whatever he stipulates he would like to have.

The plate or basket of bread of rolls may be left on the table and passed around—also the wine bottle (on a coaster, to protect the table surface).

With a small group, the dessert might be served from the host's or hostess's place, each plate filled and passed around to each guest.

The coffeepot, sugar bowl, creamer, and cups and saucers would be brought to the table and served there, after dessert, or the hosts could carry the tray into the living room, onto the patio, or wherever they wish. If the party is a big one, the easiest thing to do is to serve the coffee and the decaffeinated coffee already in the cups—and to pass the cream and sugar on the same tray as the cups.

The Cocktail Party

If you've been someone's guest for dinner, does inviting that person to a cocktail party repay one's obligation?

Not really, but it's better than nothing.

If you want eighty people actually to attend your cocktail party, how many should you invite?

In a small town, about ninety-five. In a large city, about 110 to 120. People who have to fight traffic at the end of a long business day often skip going to a cocktail party because the logistics of working it in before having to be somewhere for dinner at a certain hour are too difficult.

If there's a heavy rainstorm or snow falling, the rush-hour traffic in a large metropolis becomes impenetrable, so count on only half the people who have accepted ever making it to your party.

Are you supposed to send a thank-you note for a cocktail party?

You are not required to, but it's a *very* nice thing to do.

If you accept a cocktail party and then can't make it, do you have to do anything about it?

Yes, you should definitely call the next day to make an apology, or write a note to your hosts explaining why you couldn't get there.

How long before the cocktail party should I send out my invitations?

Two to three weeks.

What are the best hours to hold a cocktail party?

On a Saturday or Sunday, from 5 to 7. On a week night, from 5:30 to 7:30 or from 6 to 8.

I want to put "at six o'clock" as the time on my cocktail invitation, but someone said this was incorrect. Why?

If you put "at six o'clock," you're going to have a lot of guests arriving at six for cocktails and expecting a full dinner, too.

People don't RSVP cocktail-party invitations anymore, do they?

Many feel they can ignore an RSVP on a cocktail party, thinking "one more or less doesn't make any difference." However, that's being very inconsiderate of one's hosts.

Do I have to furnish cigarettes for our cocktail guests?

Ashtrays and matches, yes. Cigarettes, no.

How many drinks per guest should I plan for?

An average of three.

How many kinds of cocktails should we plan on serving at our big party?

Keep the number small. Otherwise, with a large group you'll make it very hard for the bartenders. If you're in the East, you might have Scotch as one choice; in the South, make it bourbon. Have vodka or gin. You can premix martinis the night before and refrigerate them. Forget about exotic cocktails, like gin fizzes and pink ladies. Have plenty of chilled white wine and perhaps another aperitif like sherry or Dubonnet. Have a choice of soft drinks, including low-calorie ones. For the nondrinkers, in hot weather it's also nice to have something like fresh lemonade or orangeade.

If you're having a small cocktail party, that's the time to serve Bloody Marys, or bull-shots, or daiquiris, etc.

Is it obligatory to have several kinds of hors d'oeuvres at a cocktail party?

Many people plan on "eating their dinner" at a cocktail party, and are very disappointed if the hors d'oeuvres aren't good. You should have at least one hot one, three or four cold ones, and platters of something like cold raw vegetables. You don't have to serve complicated food, but there should be enough to satisfy people who have worked hard all day and who need something to help counteract the effects of alcohol intake.

How should a bartender and waitress be dressed?

The bartender should wear a black jacket, trousers, shoes and socks, white shirt, and black tie. In the summer, he wears the same, except that his jacket is white. A waitress should wear a black uniform with a white apron in winter, a pastel uniform with a white apron in summer.

If you have college students as your bartender and waitress, a clean white shirt and black tie for the bartender and a plain black dress or black blouse and skirt for the waitress are fine. Make a request of "no running shoes or sneakers, please."

How do you know when you need a bartender and a waitress?

A couple used to entertaining can easily handle a group of twenty or so friends, particularly since their friends will make their own drinks the second time around.

If more guests than that are expected, the hosts wouldn't be able to enjoy their own party, they would be working so hard. A bartender is needed. If fifty or more are expected, two bartenders and a waitress are needed. If a hundred are expected, three bartenders and two waitresses are needed.

Is there some kind of checklist available for arranging a successful cocktail party?

You might try this one:

1. Invitations: mailed or telephoned at least two weeks prior to the event.

2. Guest parking logistics solved.
3. Children (small) and pets to be "farmed out" for the evening at friends' homes.
4. Bartenders and waitresses contacted and told how to dress.
5. Liquor ordered.
6. Ice delivery arranged.
7. Glasses, large serving trays, and coatrack rental arranged.
8. Paper napkins and hors d'oeuvres toothpicks purchased.
9. Grocery-store list ordered: soft drinks, club soda, tonic water, olives, lemons, limes, nuts, pretzels, etc. Also, all of the food for the making of hors d'oeuvres.
10. The hors d'oeuvres "chef" contracted for.
11. The household serving containers cleaned and polished.

Party Day

12. House put in order

    Furniture moved out of the way

    House cleaned to perfection

    Coat hangers in empty closet

    Ashtrays distributed everywhere

    Guest bathroom ready, with paper guest hand towels, guest soaps, etc.

    Bric-a-brac removed; valuable objets d'art put away

13. Bar area ready

    Water pitchers and glasses in place

    Trays lined up; cocktail napkins ready to go

    Soft drinks and soda water in place

    Plates of cut-up lemon rinds and lemon and lime sections ready

    Bottle opener and corkscrew (for wine bottles) ready

    Bar knife available for future fruit cutting

    Large container to hold the ice that was delivered (so it doesn't leak through the bags onto the floor)

    A few towels for each bartender.

What do you do when your cocktail party drags on, and the heavy drinkers just won't leave?

If your invitations read "6 to 8," close down the bar at 8:15. Watch the heavy drinkers leave.

Housewarming and Open House

What's the difference between an open house and a housewarming?

An open house is an invitation to friends to drop by for a period of time for refreshments. During the week, an open house is usually held at the cocktail hour, from 6 to 8. On weekends, it may be earlier in the afternoon.

A housewarming is an open house that is also the first party given in one's new home. The real fun comes from the mixing of the generations. One should have games and activities arranged for the younger generation at these parties to make them really successful. A volleyball game in the backyard into which the younger generation can drop in and out, musical tapes playing in the family room, the Ping-Pong table set up, and other distractions are nice. It's a good idea, too, to employ a teenager to organize the little ones into games during the time their parents are at the party.

It's nice to have special food, such as an "ice-cream parlor" where the young people can make their own sundaes. A portable popcorn machine is always a big hit, too.

Do I have to bring a present when I go to a housewarming?

It's nice to bring something, but the "something" does not have to be costly or grandiose. Anything from a set of gift matches to notepads for the telephones constitutes a housewarming present.

The Tea Party

I want to give a tea party at Christmas when my daughter comes home for vacation from college. I'll invite her young woman friends and my own. Since I've never had a party like this before, I would appreciate some suggestions. Also, how should we dress?

A tea party is an old-fashioned idea, but a very nice one—as well as a wonderful way for a young woman to catch up with her former high-school classmates.

You should not use tea bags for a party like this. If you don't have a silver tea service and large tray, borrow one. Have everything beautifully polished. Invite everyone for four o'clock.

Cover the dining-room table with your prettiest cloth. Put a pretty floral centerpiece on the table and several lit tapers.

On the silver tray would be the teapot on an alcohol lamp, and another pot of boiling water over another alcohol lamp (for guests who like their tea weak). There would be a basin for tea leaves, a silver sugar bowl with tongs, and a silver pitcher of milk. (Also, a container of a sugar substitute.) Arrange slices of lemon prettily on a plate, with a small fork.

It's nice to ask friends to pour on a rotating system, so that you and your daughter can talk and circulate.

Place stacks of tea plates (dessert or salad plates) on the table, dessert forks symmetrically arranged, and prettily folded napkins. The food should look very attractive—dainty sandwiches, cookies, iced cakes, and mints.

As for the proper dress for an occasion like this, you and your daughter should wear your prettiest cocktail dresses, and your guests daytime dresses or suits.

The Bridge Party

I'm giving my first bridge party. What are the things I should look out for?

Be sure that each bridge table has an easy-to-play-on surface, even if it means buying a bridge-table cover or two. Be sure the chairs for all players are comfortable, too, with good back supports.

Give each table two good clean packs of cards, four score pads, and four well-sharpened pencils with erasers.

There should be a good book of current rules on hand for reference in case of an argument.

All players should have good light with which to see their cards and the table. It helps if there's a small table for every two players on which to keep ashtrays, smoking paraphernalia, and drinks.

If you serve the players something like a gooey dessert before they sit down to play, give them moist towelettes to wipe off all stickiness on their fingers before touching the cards. Be sure there are plenty of cocktail napkins around and about their drinks, so that the moisture does not get on their fingers and consequently on the cards.

Family Swimming-Pool Party

We were forced into having to forbid people from "dropping in on us" to use our pool. Things had reached a point where we were really being taken advantage of. Now, after our firm edict, we feel that once a summer we should throw a big family party at the pool, so we won't have to feel guilty. Any ideas on the subject would be appreciated.

Send out invitations (one to a family, but with each member's name on the envelope) in which you spell out the exact time of the party, such as "from 11 to 2, with lunch at 12:30." Young children become very impatient for food unless they know in advance that food won't appear until a specific hour.

Set up a bar for the adults and a soda bar for the younger generation. A charcoal-grilling operation of hamburgers and hot dogs makes the food service easy. Have a big wholesome salad, and two kinds of dessert: platters full of half-grapefruits and melon slices, and a freezer full of ice-cream bars.

Hire a college-student swimmer to organize ballgames for the children in the water. Also swimming races and diving competitions for different age groups. Have nice prizes on hand, too, to be given out at a special awards ceremony at the end of the party.

Borrow floating equipment for the pool if you don't already have items like balls, rubber toys, and mattresses.

Have an emergency cabinet poolside, filled with items like extra pairs of sunglasses, swim caps, sun-protection lotion, paper tissue for runny noses, plastic bandages, and anything to keep people—and you—from having to go repeatedly back into the house.

If your family swimming party is held in the evening, a wonderful thing to do after dinner when it's dark is to put up a big screen by the pool and show a movie. It makes a grand finale to your party.

When making out your guest list for this kind of party, give priority to those families who do not have access to a swimming pool. Your party will be more than just "a treat" for them.

The Picnic

I think picnics are a great way to entertain. One of our friends has parties "al fresco" constantly, but with very modern, expensive, and fancy picnic equipment. Our family looks like a bunch of nomads crossing the desert when we picnic. Do we dare give a picnic party our way?

Without any hesitation. What matter at a picnic are: how well you've prepared it, how good your food tastes, and how bright your spirit is. None of that has anything to do with fancy, elegant picnic equipment.

Use a big laundry hamper or basket to carry your bottles of soda, liquor, and wine, carefully wrapped in beach towels and your tablecloths. Be sure to bring more ice containers than you could imagine using, and go through your checklist the night before the picnic (so that an emergency trip to the store can be made for anything of importance). This checklist might include the following:

1. A first-aid kit, including plenty of insect repellent, sun lotion, adhesive bandages, and a snakebite kit if you're in rattler country.
2. Bottle openers and corkscrews.
3. Condiments, sauces, and salad dressings.
4. Sugar and sweetener for coffee or tea.
5. Beer, liquor, wine, soda, iced tea, whatever you will be drinking at any point in the day.
6. Charcoal, charcoal lighting fluid, or whatever you're

using for cooking. If you're using a portable grill, put it by the door, where you'll fall over it and not leave it behind.

7. "Linens," which may be of paper, too. Don't forget the paper towels.

8. Plates (of paper or your best china, according to your mood); mugs, wineglasses, flatware.

9. Plastic bags with ties for leftovers and for garbage.

10. Several boxes or packets of matches.

11. Sunglasses, beach hats, and a beach umbrella.

12. Lightweight card tables and light collapsible chairs, if you're big on creature comforts.

13. Music: your radio, cassette player, guitar.

14. Camera and film to record this memorable scene.

15. Sports equipment—balls, bats, running shoes, fishing poles.

16. Moist towelettes for sticky hands.

17. If it's just the family, not a party, there should be a good book for everyone to read.

The menu can be anything from delicious hamburgers to a memorable stew that only has to be reheated. Or you can cook everything at home and transport it, ready to eat, without lighting a fire, such as this menu for a hot, sizzling day:

Cold cream-of-vegetable soup (made in your blender)
Brown bread, thinly buttered and cut into four squares
   per slice
Broiled chicken quarters (made just before leaving home
   and still warm in their foil wrap)
Cold rice salad
Fresh-fruit compote with brownies
White wine, well-chilled

Epilogue to any picnic: Clean your campsite so beautifully, no one will know you were ever there. If there are large containers on the spot for trash, fine. Otherwise, bring it home. Dispose of *nothing* on the beach, in the woods, in the water.

Put out any fire you have made, and pour water on the logs until there is absolutely no sign of steam. Never camouflage burning coals on the beach by throwing sand over them; someone could badly burn his feet by walking over it.

Good manners in nature are esssential; otherwise, there will be no nature for our descendants to enjoy.

Being a Host—and Being a Guest —for the Weekend

We have rented a house on a lake. What should we as hosts keep in mind as we organize our schedule of weekend guests?

For one thing, invite your friends one to two months ahead, so they won't be busy doing something else when you want them.

Invite couples who would fit in with each other. (In other words, don't invite a pair of screaming liberals with a pair of archconservatives, don't invite a pair who plays bridge *every* night of their lives with a pair who never plays bridge *any* night of their lives.)

Be very specific about when you want them to arrive and when you want them to leave. Say something like, "We'll expect you before dinner Friday, and hope you'll stay through the cocktail hour on Sunday." Be knowledgeable about schedules of trains and buses that pass near your home, the airlines that fly into a nearby airport, etc. Have a map made to show how to get to your house, if it's complicated.

Send your guests a possible list of activities and what to bring along to wear. For example, "We might go to the club dance Saturday, so bring a black tie and a long dress. . . . I also ought to warn you that the tennis committee allows only whites on the courts."

You might have a different clothes story to tell: "Don't bring anything dressy. We won't be out of shorts or pants the entire weekend. No jackets or ties necessary."

Whatever the dress requirements, communicate them. Warn your guests if the weather at that time of year gets chilly, or if it's really very hot.

The Guestroom. Here's a checklist of conditions observed by a good host before subjecting a guest to a night in the guestroom:

The Necessities
1. Are the beds comfortable? Equipped with enough blankets and pillows? Mattresses in good condition?

2. Do the windows go up and down? Are the screens in good condition? Does the room need a fan?

3. Does the room have a large wastebasket? Is there one also in the bathroom?

4. Does each bed have a good reading lamp with a high-wattage bulb?

5. If your guests are smokers, are there sufficient matches and ashtrays in the room?

6. Is the closet clean, and does it contain several kinds of hangers?

7. Are the bureau drawers empty and lined with clean shelf paper?

8. If possible, have a clock-radio in the room.

9. Have a notepad and pen on the desk, and nice stationery and postcards inside the desk.

10. Make sure there are some good books and magazines in the room.

The Niceties (extras that are frosting on the cake)

1. A bouquet of flowers or a pretty little plant on the bureau.

2. A small TV set.

3. A tray on the bureau holding a good woman's fragrance and a man's cologne.

4. A sewing kit in the bureau drawer.

5. A small ironing board and iron in the closet.

6. An airtight tin of "goodies" for someone with a sweet tooth.

7. A thermos pitcher of ice water.

8. A tray on the closet shelf containing a coffeemaker with a tin of coffee, a covered sugar bowl, two spoons, and two pretty coffeecups and saucers.

Organizing the Guest Bathroom

1. Women should have a good light with which to put on their makeup, and men need a good light with which to shave.

2. Separate, well-supplied towel racks are needed for each guest.

3. Don't forget a shower cap.

4. Hooks on the back of the door are needed to hold dressing gowns and nightclothes.

5. Make sure the medicine cabinet is well supplied with: Fresh toothbrushes

Toothpaste
Deodorant
Razor and packet of blades
Shampoo
Hair spray
New comb
Package of hair clips
Box of adhesive bandages
Bottle of insect repellent for a resort house
Suntanning lotion

6. Place on rim of the tub a small container of detergent and a new sponge for cleaning the tub.
7. On a small table, include the following:
Hand lotion
Bath powder
Extra roll of toilet tissue
Box of paper tissues
Mild soap powder for personal laundry
Electric hair dryer

Is it better to organize your guests or leave them totally free?

It depends on your guests. If they tell you they're exhausted and are "longing to collapse," leave them alone.

If they're athletically inclined, reserve tennis courts for them, arrange their schedules to allow plenty of time to play their particular sports.

Post a schedule of when and where meals will be served and any special dress instructions.

Figure out their transportation to and from various activities. This might include coordinating everything from a rented car to a friend's borrowed car, and from a bicycle to a mo-ped.

For the churchgoers, post the address of the church and the hours of the services.

What should a person do to be considered "a desirable guest," one who will be welcomed back next year?

Don't bring your children uninvited.
Leave your pets at home.
Arrive on time, leave on time, never stay over "for just another day."

Don't arrive sick. Cancel. No one likes to run a sick ward for a guest.

Bring a tasteful, useful present—like food or liquor or a great new family game.

Keep your quarters very neat and tidy. Offer "to help anytime," but don't keep sounding like a broken record, repeating, almost whining an offer to help your hosts.

Arrive well equipped, including with your own tennis and golf balls.

Keep off your host's telephone; when you call long distance, use your credit card or pay back your host immediately.

Be on time, properly dressed, for every part of the schedule.

If you break something, report it and replace it.

Be considerate to all members of the host's family.

Write a warm, personal letter of thanks to your hosts after the weekend, mention details of things that pleased you.

If you didn't bring a "hostess present," send one after your return home.

The Teen Party

Do people still give "sweet-sixteen" parties for their children?

It's still a big party occasion in some people's lives. Many children receive their driver's licenses on this birthday, and some parents do give a special party for classmates of both sexes. They don't necessarily call it, however, a sweet-sixteen party, because that title antagonizes some teenagers!

Some parents prefer to wait until their child reaches his or her eighteenth birthday to give a big party, which then becomes a good-bye-to-high-school, hello-to-college, and now-we-can-serve-liquor-legally party.

When a young high-school student gives a party at home, how does a parent keep drugs and alcohol out of it? Our daughter says if we are going to be strict about this, no one will come to her birthday party.

You can make the party sound so enticing, they'll all come. You can make the party so much fun with so many activities, they won't care that drugs and alcohol aren't part of it. They won't be bored, so they won't miss the artificial highs.

Lay down the rules carefully—right on the invitations. Have them specially designed, give the party a special name, mention that a band will be present, a treasure hunt, a fortune-teller, and other surprises. But add on the invitation: "no pot, no booze," or whatever vernacular you wish to use.

Hire a college athletic hero and his or her date to chaperone the event. The young people will respect the "older" young people, particularly when they are recognized as superior athletes. When a college swimming star, for example, says to someone who is caught pouring liquor into young people's drinks, "What are you doing with that stuff? Put it away. Not here. That stuff is absolute poison to your body. You couldn't swim a yard with that stuff in you," the high-school students listen.

College "chaperones" can keep your party clean of all that "poison," whereas you, the parents, probably can't.

Hire a good trio from a college or music school to play dance music. Or hire a professional disc jockey. Have a treasure hunt indoors or outdoors. Have a magician doing tricks, a fortune-teller doing her stuff with her magic crystal or reading the tea leaves. Have a contest with segments of "mystery voices" from records played briefly, and the guests who guess accurately the greatest number of singers' names receive prizes. Have a dance contest. Have lots of good food and soft drinks. Make the evening so full of action and excitement, your daughter's guests will think this is the greatest party they have ever attended in their lives.

It may well be—so far.

Table Manners

What's the difference between eating "American-style" and "continental-style," and which way is better?

In the American system, when cutting one's food, one holds the fork in the left hand and the knife in the right hand.

Then one puts down the knife and transfers the fork from the left to the right hand for the purpose of putting food on the fork and into the mouth.

In the continental system, one holds the fork in the left hand and the knife in the right for cutting purposes, and also for eating purposes. One continues to hold the knife in the right hand, and the fork therefore stays in the left hand. There is no useless shifting of utensils. The knife also contains the food—in a support system—until a morsel is safely on the fork.

I feel the continental system is best, and everyone uses it except the Americans. We have tried to find out through research when and why the American system of holding the fork in the right hand came into being. The answer has not yet surfaced.

What do you do with your fork and knife when you've finished eating?

Place them side by side in the middle of your plate, the fork tines up or down, the knife to its right, sharp blade pointed inward toward the fork.

I know you are supposed to leave your dessert fork and spoon on the plate when you're finished, but if the dessert bowl is very big and doesn't leave enough room on the rim of the underplate, isn't it better to leave the dessert spoon and fork in the bowl itself?

Yes. That's a logical exception to the rule of never leaving an eating utensil in a bowl, compote, or cup; if after eating there's not enough room for your utensils on the underplate, you have no choice.

What are the rules adults should remember about napkins?

The large dinner napkins need to be only half-unfolded; the smaller luncheon napkin must be spread out completely on the lap.

Never return the napkin to the table until you leave it. Even if everyone has long finished eating and people are lingering over coffee at the table, keep your napkin on your lap. Then fold it neatly and place it on the table as you leave.

To spoon up more liquid, do you tip a soup or dessert dish toward you or away from you, and is this really good manners?

Yes, if you want something delicious right down to the last drop, it is perfectly good manners to go after it. Spoon liquid *away* from you. Tip the bowl *away* from you.

If you're missing something like a fork, knife, or spoon at your place, should you ask your host for one, or should you try to make do without it?

Always ask for it.

Is it all right to pick up your soup cup or bowl and drink from it?

Yes, provided it's not a large soup *plate,* and if there isn't a lot of garnish floating on top that would make your mouth very messy. Always eat first anything floating or anything solid in a soup with your spoon; then you may pick up the container and sip its liquid. Hold it in one hand only if it has a handle.

The thing to watch out for while eating soup is making a slurping noise.

When you're holding a handled cup, like soup or tea, is it elegant to crook your little finger?

No, it's affected, and anything affected is never elegant.

How are you supposed to hold glasses?

A stemmed water or wine goblet is held with the thumb and the first two fingers at the base of the bowl. If the glass contains a chilled wine, however (white or rosé) hold the glass by its stem, so as not to heat the wine with your fingers on the bowl.

Hold a tumbler near its base.

What size food portion are you supposed to take?

Medium-size. If you really like something and take a big portion, you are in danger of being called greedy; you also might be taking someone else's portion. If you take too small a portion, it looks as if you don't like your hostess's food.

How do you use chopsticks?

When a serving platter is passed with something extra under the main course being served, are you supposed to take it, or just the meat?

Take it all. If there's a piece of toast under a piece of meat, for example, or a toasted muffin, you pick up all of it together—with the serving fork and serving spoon supporting it until it makes a safe landing on your plate.

I never know how many to take when there are things like little birds, little chops, etc., on a platter.

If it's little birds, take only one; if it's minuscule lamb chops, take two; if the chicken pieces are very small, take two. If the meat is sliced, like beef tenderloin, take one piece. If you're ever in doubt, take one. The platter will be passed again.

If gravy is passed and you don't know what to put it on, what do you do?

Look at what the other guests are doing, and take your cue. If you're the first to be served, use logic: gravy is usually for meat. A cream or cheese sauce is usually for a green vegetable. If something like a strong-smelling white sauce (horseradish) is passed after you have helped yourself to roast beef or corned beef, put some next to your meat. You can dab it on the meat later.

A kind hostess often realizes a guest may be confused as to the purpose of a sauce being passed; she should casually mention, "That's my special meat sauce."

When jams and jellies are passed, I never know what to do with them, particularly when I think it's for meat and yet I have a butter plate, too.

If you have fowl or lamb or your plate, spoon some jelly onto your dinner plate. If you have a butter plate and another kind of main course is served, put the jam or jelly on the butter plate.

If you have butter on a butter plate and want to put it on your vegetables, is that all right to do?

Not when you're someone's guest. The cook is supposed to know how to add butter to the vegetables. The two exceptions are baked potatoes and corn on the cob.

Is it all right to put lots of spices on food in someone's home, if one does it in one's own home? And is it all right to ask for things like steak sauce and catsup for the meat?

Never put salt and pepper on food before tasting it. And if you're someone's guest, add salt and pepper sparingly and inconspicuously; otherwise your host will think his food was improperly prepared or tasteless. Never ask for steak sauce or catsup to go over meat prepared by your host's kitchen. It's an insult to the cook.

Is it all right to soak a bit of bread in the remnants of a delicious sauce on one's plate?

Yes, it's a compliment to the cuisine. Break off a *small* piece of bread or roll, spear it with your fork, and carefully soak up the sauce.

What do you do about left-handed guests?

Be considerate. If possible, place a left-handed guest so that he has a table end on his left side. (That's also being considerate of his right-handed neighbor!)

When you have something in your mouth you want to spit out, like an olive pit or a tough piece of gristle or a fish bone, what do you do?

Don't spit it out. Work the pit or stone or something unswallowable onto your fork or spoon with your tongue, then transfer it to the plate. If you're eating fresh cherries, hold each one by the stem, eat the cherry, and place the pit right from your mouth into your cupped hand, then onto the plate.

Is it all right to use a knife to remove a bit of food that has spilled down one's front?

Yes, but make it a *clean* knife. Then you can quickly dab at the spot with a corner of your napkin. (You may also dip the napkin corner into your glass and dab some water on the spot, if you do it quickly, quietly, and without drawing attention to yourself.)

What do you do if someone is choking on food at the table?

If that person answers, "I'm all right," to your question offering assistance, you should all go on talking and drawing attention away from the person, who is obviously embarrassed.

If the person (who looks as though he was choking or having difficulty) is unable to answer you, it's time for quick action—perhaps to save a life. Perhaps the choking guest will point to his throat, a sign anyone familiar with the Heimlich maneuver knows is the sign of choking. Quickly make that guest stand up at table; then use the Heimlich maneuver on him to dislodge whatever is stuck in his throat. (The way to help save a choking person's life may be obtained from the Life Extension Institute at 1185 Avenue of the

Americas, New York, New York 10036.) It takes only four minutes to die from choking.

If you feel a sneeze coming on at table and you have no handkerchief, what are you supposed to do?

Cover your face with your napkin, excuse yourself from the table at once, and repair to a bathroom, where you can finish blowing your nose in privacy. Remember to bring some paper tissue back to the table with you.

When someone asks you a question and your mouth is full of food, what do you do, particularly when all eyes at the table are on you?

It's up to the person who asked you the question to be considerate, to laugh, and quickly turn away from you, redirecting the question elsewhere.

If the person who asks you the question is not that considerate, just smile with your eyes and point to your mouth. Chew slowly, don't bolt your food down, and don't try to say one word with your mouth full.

If you get food stuck in your teeth, I've heard you can take out a toothpick at the table to dislodge it—provided you hold your napkin up in front of your face.

No, no toothpicks, no fingernails, no probing for food stuck in teeth when you're at the table. If you can't dislodge it with your tongue, try to get through the meal until everyone leaves the table and you can find a bathroom to repair the situation.

If you are in absolute agony over it, excuse yourself quickly from the table and take care of the situation in the bathroom. Rinsing your mouth vigorously with water will often solve the problem.

If you feel a burp coming on when you're sitting at a dinner party, what should you do?

Don't try to suppress it. Cover your nose and mouth with your napkin, and after it happens, say to no one in particular, "Excuse me."

If it looks like an attack of burps, the person should excuse himself from the table until it has passed.

If a bug crawls out of your salad or a fly lands in your iced tea, what do you do?

Fish out the fly and deposit him firmly in your napkin on your lap, without conversation about it, and as inconspicuously as possible. Snatch the nasty creature coming from your salad and dispatch him also to another life in your napkin on your lap. It would embarrass your hosts and sicken their guests if you were to point it out to them.

Why are elbows on the table considered so "terrible"?

Elbows on the table while you're eating makes you look sloppy and undisciplined. Elbows on the table in between courses are all right, provided the hands are folded and one hand isn't used as a cushion for what looks like a tired head.

A good erect posture helps you eat more gracefully and enjoy your food more. It also shows your host that you are glad to be at his table, and not tired or bored.

What do you do when someone is driving you crazy at the table by drumming his fingers on the table?

A nervous habit like that can ruin anyone else's enjoyment of a meal. Turn to your neighbor and say with a big smile on your face something only he can hear, like, "Hey, did you know you're wearing out a spot on the tablecloth with your fingers? Are you trying out for a rhythm band or something?"

The person is usually grateful for a reminder that his bad habit is showing, particularly if it is done in a friendly tone.

If you're used to saying grace at home, and you're the guest in someone's home and no grace is said, is it all right to speak up and say, "I think we ought to have grace"?

No, it's better to say your grace quietly to yourself.

We always say grace in our house, before every meal. Is it all right if we make our dinner guests say it, too?

Absolutely. If they're already seated, don't make them stand up again. Whoever is saying grace should just explain, "We always say grace in this family, so I'd like to say it right now."

Your dinner guests will like it.

A guest should follow the customs of the house, wherever he or she may be.

How to Eat Certain Foods

When you're served an artichoke, how are you supposed to eat it?

There's usually a small container of sauce, into which you dip the leaves. Pull the leaf off and eat the blunt end of it (never the sharp-pointed end) after dipping it into the sauce. Then put the used leaf onto an empty plate that may have been provided, or if not, place each leaf in a neat pile next to your artichoke.

When you reach the inner fuzzy gray part, the choke, hold it with a fork and then cut off the feathery portion with your knife. The inside "heart" is then cut into small pieces, dipped into the sauce, and eaten with gusto.

When do you eat asparagus with a knife and fork, and when with your fingers?

If the asparagus is covered by a hollandaise or a vinaigrette sauce, cut it with your knife and fork and eat all but the toughest end portions that way

If the asparagus has a minimum of butter or sauce on it, pick up the stalk and dip the ends into a sauce dish or just eat it without any sauce. You may eat it right down to the tough part of the stalk. (In season, sometimes the entire stalk is soft and edible.)

Can you eat bacon with your fingers?

Only if it's crisp and not covered with a lot of grease or a sauce.

If you're served a small bird, can you pick it up in your fingers?

Try to cut off some pieces of meat first. Then pick it up.

Should chicken be eaten with the fingers?

If you're on a picnic or at a backyard barbecue, everyone eats chicken quite properly with their fingers. But if you're in someone's home as a guest, use a fork and knife until you are unable to cut off any more. Watch your hosts. If they pick up their pieces of chicken "at the end," you may certainly do likewise, to get at those last delicate, hard-to-reach morsels of chicken on the bone.

If you're eating roast or fried chicken at a party when you're in dinner clothes, forget about picking up your chicken. Why risk ruining your clothes with grease marks?

And, of course, if the chicken is cooked in a casserole sauce, it is *never* picked up.

Is it all right to serve corn on the cob at a dinner party?

Since corn on the cob is so messy to eat, it is more considerate to serve your dinner-party guests corn *off* the cob. Corn on the cob is a welcome addition to a beach party, a backyard barbecue, anything very informal where one is dressed in clothes "that can take it."

How do you eat small fish?

They are delicious when they are cleaned, fried, and served whole.

Cut off the head, spear the fish with your fork, and slit it from the head to the tail with the tip of your knife. Open it out flat, and then with the tip of your knife under one end of the backbone and with your fork helping at the other end, lift up the backbone (and most of the tiny bones with it) right out from the fish. Lay the skeleton on the outer edge of your plate, cut the rest of the fish with a knife and fork, and enjoy it.

How do you approach a plateful of steamed clams?

If the shell is difficult to open, abandon that clam. The others with easy-to-open shells are good ones. Take the clam out by its little neck with two fingers of one hand, while you hold the shell in your other hand. Then loosen the neck skin covering from the clam and discard that piece. The clam should be all slippery now; dip it in melted butter and then in clam broth, or in just one of those two liquids.

The hosts should provide a large bowl into which one tosses all empty clam shells. There's also a need for extra napkins at a clam feast, and for reserve moist towelettes or finger bowls to handle the sticky fingers.

What if you've never had a whole lobster before? Will I be able to eat one at a dinner party and not humiliate myself?

The host is supposed to crack well the claws of a lobster or a hard-shelled crab before serving it to a guest, so don't worry. The cracker you will be furnished is just to apply the final pressure to make the lobster shell crack open easily. You will also be given a small oyster fork or a nut pick to extract the delicious meat from the small claws and crevices. Each time you have a nice piece of meat on your fork, dip it in melted butter and then eat it. If you're careful in extracting the large-claw meat, it will come out in a whole piece and will require cutting.

You'll find green material (called the tomalley) in the stomach cavity, and the "coral" or roe in the female. Some people eat them; others prefer not to.

Pull the small claws away from the body and suck the ends of them to extract their delicate meat and juice.

How are mussels eaten?

They may be passed to you at a cocktail party on a toothpick, pickled or smoked. Eat the mussel right off the toothpick. If you are served *moules marinières* as a first course, you will find a wonderful garlicky soup with the mussels present in their open shells. You may pick them out of their shells with the little fork or pick. You may also pick up the shell and suck out the mussel and its juice from the shell. Often there's a bowl provided for the empty shells. Use a soup spoon to consume the excellent broth that remains after the mussels are eaten.

What is the proper way to eat clams and oysters?

Hold the oyster or clam shell in your left hand, and using an oyster fork, lift the oyster or clam whole from the shell, helping detach it, if necessary, with your fork. Dip it into the sauce provided nearby, but sometimes lemon juice or a special sauce will have already been put on them.

It's perfectly all right to pick up the shell and suck out all its juice after you have eaten its contents.

What do you do if each shrimp in the shrimp cocktail is too big to be eaten in one bite? Cut it with a knife and fork?

No, because you can't wield a knife in a small shrimp-cocktail compote. Take a shrimp on your fork and bite off a small portion on the end. Then bite off another portion, dipping it in the sauce each time, of course, if you wish to.

If you're someone's guest for dinner at home and pizza is served, does it have to be eaten with a fork and knife?

It's neater that way, but watch your hosts. Pizza is a very informal food, and it almost tastes better when eaten with the fingers!

Can you pick up french fries, potato chips, and shoestring potatoes with your fingers when you're at a dinner party?

Yes, provided they're not all greasy or accidentally swimming in a sauce that's on the plate. If the french fries are enormous, it's better to eat them with a fork, under any circumstances.

Is it all right to cut your salad?

Absolutely. Some pieces of lettuce are too overpowering for a fork.

If you're attacking a triple-decker sandwich that is really big, how can it be eaten?

Take each quarter of the triple-decker, open it up with your knife and fork, and then cut the now doubled sections into manageable bites, which you eat with a fork, not your fingers. You know, the more you get used to using your fork and knife to cut and eat, the more difficult it becomes to use the fingers.

When sherbet is served with a salad or with a piece of fowl, I never know what utensil to use to eat it.

Use either a fork or a spoon. If the only spoon at your place is destined for dessert, however, eat it with your fork.

What's the genuine, authentic way of eating spaghetti, Italian-style?

You take just a few strands, twine them around your fork, and keep turning, turning until the long strands are all neatly wound around the fork. Then it goes into the mouth. A novice may need to use a large spoon as a buttressing operation during the turning operation. A piece of bread held in the opposite hand can also help the novice keep the spaghetti neatly on the fork.

Cutting spaghetti with a fork is enough to sadden a true pasta cook's heart.

Is it all right to eat tortillas with your fingers?

It's practically the only way. A tortilla filled with something like frijoles (kidney beans) is rolled up and eaten like a hot dog.

Is it polite to eat a whole piece of bread, or does it have to be cut in smaller pieces? Is it all right to butter the whole piece at once? And is it all right to stick one's breadstick into the butter so that the end is delightfully buttery?

You may butter your whole piece of bread or your roll before eating it. A piece of bread or toast should then be cut in half before eating it, however. It is certainly all right to stick a breadstick into one's butter, too.

If you take a sticky bun, be sure to cut it in half before eating it.

What do you think of people who reach over to sample the food from someone else's plate? And who drink from someone else's beverage glass?

People should order and take what they want. They should not reach over to sample other people's food. If a group at a special restaurant wishes to sample different dishes they should order a varied menu, and then, before anyone has raised a fork to the mouth, they should section off samples on their plates and give those samples to anyone interested.

It's unsanitary to use anyone else's cup or glass.

When a bowl of fresh fruit is passed, may one take more than one choice? It there a special etiquette for eating this fruit?

The bowl of fruit offered at the end of a meal is meant to be enjoyed. You may certainly take more than one thing, but without appearing gluttonous.

When you take an apple or a pear, you may want to remove the skin first, with your knife, in a circular motion. Then cut the piece of fruit into halves, remove the core, and then quarter the fruit. Take a small portion of grapes (use the grape shears to cut off what you want, if there is a pair of shears tucked into the bowl).

After eating a fruit with a substantial stone, like an apricot or a plum, transfer the stone from your mouth onto the fork that is raised to your lips, and then onto the plate.

If you take a banana, peel it and cut it into small pieces with your fruit fork and knife. (If you're on a picnic, you eat a banana whole.)

A ripe mango should be cut in half with a sharp fruit knife, and then quartered. Pull up a bit of skin, hold that piece with a fork, and pull off the rest of the skin. Cut up the juicy part of the fruit into small pieces.

A papaya should be halved, the black seeds removed, and then eaten like any melon.

Can one serve fresh pineapple with the skin on?

It's too difficult for most people to manage. Remove the spiny outer skin in the kitchen and serve it in even slices.

When you're eating a peach, should you peel it first?

If you like. Before peeling it, cut it in half, then quarter it and pull off the skin of each section.

Is it all right to serve a guest a grapefruit half that has not been cut into sections?

No, that is not being considerate. Cut all the little sections with a sharp knife in the kitchen. A guest in good clothes would be at a disadvantage in having to cut the grapefruit.

How are tangerines and oranges eaten?

Use your knife and cut off the top of the orange or tangerine. Often the rest of the skin will come off easily in your fingers. If you have a stubborn orange skin, peel it carefully with a knife, so that orange juice doesn't squirt in all directions.

Part the sections of the orange or the tangerine with your fingers. Remove the pulpy strings from the fruit, and then eat it with your fork, section by section.

Business Etiquette

Applying for a Job

How do "good manners" pertain to a successful job hunt?

Well, for one thing, if you don't show good manners on the telephone and in your letter requesting the interview, you're never going to get that interview.

For another thing, good manners greatly impress an interviewer, who then logically concludes, "Here is someone who is well-mannered and who would get along well with people, both within and without our organization."

Manners are a tremendous asset. They make a person stand out in the crowd.

Is there a well-mannered way of acting in the interview?

When you're brought into the interviewer's office, wait right where you are if the other person is reading a report or talking on the telephone. Wait for a signal of when to talk and when to sit down and where.

Your first words to the interviewer should be: "Thank you so much for agreeing to see me."

When seated by the interviewer's desk, don't loll over it. Sit up straight (no slumping, with legs in a sprawl). If you still have to wait before the interviewer can leave the business at hand and turn to you, don't pick up anything on the desk or try to read anything lying there. When the interviewer finally talks to you, look him or her straight in the eye; answer succinctly and honestly every question.

Does how you're dressed have any effect?

Absolutely—even if the others in the office are dressed in a very informal, relaxed manner. A man on an interview should look immaculately clean in his conservative suit and tie. A woman should look immaculately clean in her conservative suit or dress. Hair should be well-groomed, the hands and nails clean. Shoes should be well-shined. A woman's makeup should be understated and subtle—so should her jewelry and fragrance.

An interviewer tends to feel that people who don't care about their appearance wouldn't care about their jobs or about their company, either.

What is the polite thing to do after the interview?

Write a letter of thanks immediately to the interviewer, expressing your interest in the job and your appreciation for the time given you. Tell in your own words how much it would mean to be employed by "such a wonderful company."

Be sure also to write a thank-you to anyone who allowed you to use him as a reference in applying for a job, or to anyone who made a call or wrote a letter on your behalf.

Shouldn't the interviewer show some manners too?

Yes, and one of the most important ways an interviewer shows *his* or *her* good manners is to write a nice letter to the job applicant when the position has been filled by another candidate.

It is very hard on someone who thinks he's being seriously considered for a job when that job has already been taken by someone else. The firm doing the hiring has the responsibility to communicate disappointing news quickly and kindly to everyone who felt he or she was in the running.

What are the points to remember in writing a letter of reference for someone who is trying to get a job?

If you are strongly recommending that person, make your letter an enthusiastic one, full of glowing praise. If you have some reservations about the person, express them in a qualified way, not in a brusque negative way (the latter might assure that the person will never get a job anywhere).

Here are examples of qualified references:

"Although Jim Nelson is not yet an accomplished reports writer, he has good ability with the graphs, tables, and supporting-visuals aspects of the project." ... "Although Mrs. Simpson is not as talented in the administrative field as she is in her individual contributions, her work for us was very fine."

How do you write a proper letter of resignation?

Non-executive personnel address their letters to the head of personnel (or human resources, or whatever it's called). An executive would write to his or her chief executive officer.

The letter should be dated, and should include the date the resignation will become effective, as well as the reasons why. It is better not to unburden yourself of your feelings of vitriol toward the company or toward certain people within it. It is far better to submit an innocuous resignation letter, so that you won't be rejected by a future employer as a "hothead" or a troublemaker when your letter is taken from the files to be read. Following is a "gentle" letter of resignation that does not contain the drama and bad behavior that went on behind the corporate scene at the time:

Dear Mr. Adams:

It is with great regret that after twelve happy years of affiliation with the C. Z. Adams Company, I must submit my resignation. It will take effect July 1, 1982.

Personal family considerations have made my resignation advisable, particularly since an opportunity with the XYZ Company has presented itself. The new job has such a great potential for the future, it was impossible to refuse.

I shall greatly miss my fellow officers and this company, an organization I view with respect and affection. I would like to express to you, the board of directors, and the entire staff of the C. Z. Adams Company every good wish for continued success in the future.

Sincerely,
John Smith

Men and Women's Relationships

Who do you think is having the more difficult time—women or men—in adjusting to the new world where women have jobs that were traditionally held by men?

Both are uncomfortable. Women who are succeeding in these new territories, in holding different kinds of jobs, often don't know how to comport themselves with their male colleagues. They are criticized if they copy a man's masculine, aggressive behavior. They're criticized if they play it quiet and low-key, because then "they're too soft to know how to be tough enough." If they're too crisp and businesslike, they are called a "masculine kind of woman," and if they are ultra-feminine, they are sometimes accused of "using sex as a weapon of success."

Many men don't know how to react to these new women in their midst; and the women don't know how to interrelate either. Time will be the answer. As more women step up into top jobs in the corporate and industrial worlds, everyone will become more relaxed and learn simply to work with each other on a person-to-person basis, not on a gender-to-gender basis. In the meantime, we should have patience and show great consideration to one another.

What kind of traditions does the executive man have to abandon in his dealings with the new executive woman?

Such "acts of chivalry," for example, as always picking up the check in a restaurant; of helping a woman with her coat; of feeling compelled to rush ahead to hold the door for her; of standing up when a woman arrives late in the meeting, and then helping seat her; of getting off the elevator last in order to allow the women behind to leave the car first.

If a man has been trained, exactly as the men have been trained in his family generations before, to treat women with great deference, why should he be expected to change?

Because a woman feels that a man who always treats her like a fragile flower is not going to let her make any tough decisions in the boardroom. In fact, he's not even going to let her inside the door of the boardroom unless she's going to decorate it or take dictation in it!

How does the new world of manners work, then?

People help each other when help is needed. If a man is going down the corridor with his arms loaded with books and files, a woman behind him should rush ahead to open and hold the door for him. He would do the same for her.

When hunting for a taxi, whoever has an arm free hails the cab. It does *not* have to be the man who does it. A woman puts on her own coat, and a man puts on his own coat, but if either of them is having trouble getting on the coat, because of things being carried, one should quickly move to help the other with the coat.

The new world of manners is a logical give-and-take, help-each-other-when-help-is-needed kind of society toward which we hopefully are working together.

Business-Greeting Etiquette

When a man arrives from outside the company for an appointment with a woman executive, does she remain seated when he enters her office?

No. A woman executive rises from her chair and walks toward her visitor, her hand extended for a handshake. She shows him to his chair and sits down after he does. A man executive acts the same when a woman executive comes into his office, and men and women executives act the same way when someone of their own sex arrives for an appointment.

Each executive should accompany his or her visitor to the elevators at the end of the appointment—or at least to the reception area.

What about officers in your own company when they walk into your office? You don't have to keep bobbing up and down for them, do you?

Even if you are a senior executive, when the chairman or the company president enters your office for the *first time that day,* you should rise from your desk out of respect. You do not have to do it again.

Young executives should automatically stand up when any senior officer of any sex enters the office, but again, the first time is enough. You don't have to make a big thing out of it. A quick rise, a motion to the other person to sit, and you've done your well-mannered duty.

Should one say "sir" to a senior man as a mark of respect?

If you've been trained since childhood to do it, continue. It is no longer a required part of a young man's vocabulary when he's addressing a senior man. Today it's better to call him by name—"Mr. Smith" or "Dr. Cantwell"—instead of "sir." It's more efficient, and less obsequious.

As for a woman executive, never call her "ma'am."

When do you start calling your senior executives by their first names?

Only when they instruct you to. Never start it first; never ask if they would please call you "Bob" so you can call them "Rick" and "George."

Even if you are on a first-name basis with someone like the president of the company, if you pass him when he's in the company of clients from the outside, don't be familiar with him and call him by his first name. It's better to say "Good morning, Mrs. Johnson," or "Hello, Mr. Erickson."

A business such as a bank or any place that deals with great amounts of the public's money likes to maintain a formal and serious atmosphere when clients are present. The client is more likely to trust an institution with his or her own money when an attitude of discipline prevails.

Why use "Ms." anyway? What's wrong with "Miss"?

"Miss" refers to someone who has never married. "Ms." refers to a woman of any marital status, just as "Mr." refers to a man of any marital status—single, married, divorced, or widowed.

"Ms." is very helpful and efficient in business. It saves one time. One does not have to call a woman's office when addressing a letter to her to find out if she's "Miss" or "Mrs."

In business the use of "Ms." is a time-saver. In social situations, it's also a step toward equality.

Secretaries and Their Bosses

As an executive secretary, I call my boss by his last name. It's company policy. Why can't I therefore insist on his calling me by my last name?

You should be able to. Ask him nicely. Explain how you feel about it. Most executives don't even realize this creates a problem, and once it's pointed out, they quickly adjust.

I'm sick of being a "gofer" for my two bosses. All I seem to do is get their coffee and do their personal shopping—errands that should be run by their wives. I am ready for a nasty rebellion.

Abandon any plan of a "rebellion." Be reasonable, and talk it out with both bosses. Suggest that the fetching of the coffee and other similar duties within the office be shared by several people, and that they themselves take a turn at getting the coffee every other week or so. As for the personal shopping, explain it really isn't part of your job and that you would perform your office duties far more successfully if you didn't have to cope with those personal items.

Then suggest you'd be happy to do the personal shopping on weekends, if you could be properly compensated for it.

My boss has given me, his secretary, some lingerie as a present. I'm in a quandary to know what to do.

Don't be in a quandary. Return it at once to him, and tell him your own version of "Thanks, but no thanks."

I feel my secretary deserves a higher status than she enjoys in this organization. What do you suggest I do?

Promote her, for one thing. Raise her salary and change her title to something you like, such as "executive assistant," "executive office coordinator," or "administrative coordinator."

Give her some more privileges—such as permission to use the executive dining room at lunch.

Why do so many men keep referring to their secretaries as "my girl" or "my girl Friday"?

Because their secretaries haven't asked them to stop doing it. Again, most men do not realize the offense that this gives, and they would cease immediately if their secretaries explained to them why they consider it demeaning. (A boss would never, for example, refer to his male secretary as "my boy," so why do it to a woman!)

Is a secretary supposed to rise from his or her desk to greet the boss's visitor?

If the secretary is not handling two telephones at once, transcribing dictation, or otherwise totally distracted, he or she should rise to greet the visitor from the outside. It is a mark of respect. It pleases the visitor and reflects well on the organization.

Dress in the Office

How should a person dress for a job?

It depends on the nature of the business, the dictates of fashion, the size and shape of the person, and the life-style of the area. People in Southern California dress so casually, their dress codes for what is proper to wear to work are entirely different from those of the Northeast.

Here is a list of questions to ask yourself:

1. Is the office I'm going to work for conservative, like a bank, or will I be working with a free-wheeling

group, like the art department of an ad agency or a small architectural office?
2. *How is everyone else dressed in that office?*
3. Do I have the figure and shape to wear the "latest" fashions?
4. Even if everyone dresses in resort clothes, would I feel more comfortable and do better at my job if I dressed a little more formally, conservatively?

How does grooming affect one's career?

Importantly. A badly groomed person looks as though he or she doesn't care about his or her own person, as well as the company.

Are pants on women always appropriate?

If they are well cut and if the woman's figure warrants wearing them. There are places, of course, where they do not look well—such as if the executives go to a good restaurant to dine after a work session—the kind of restaurant where everyone is more or less formally attired. A woman in tailored daytime slacks would look out-of-place there. Also if she is attending a colleague's wedding (or funeral!).

What if your good friend wears sexy, low-cut dresses to work —do you warn her what people are saying about her?

Yes, in a kind way. Don't tell her that her clothes are provocative and leading her nowhere except into a bad reputation and toward a loss of job promotions. Instead show her some new fashion-magazine pages of conservative, smart clothes, and suggest that her superiors have been heard to remark that such a "look" is more in fashion for the office than the costumes she has been wearing.

Your friend should get the hint—and take it, if she cares about her job.

Having the Right Attitude as One Begins the Job

I'm starting a job in an office for the first time. What are some of the things to remember, in order to make a good impression?

Here's my own list, learned from hard experience when I began my first job:

Offer to run errands for others if you're going out, such as bringing back lunch, buying stamps, fetching needed office supplies.

When you borrow anything, always return it immediately, and in good shape. Never borrow money in the office.

Leave your desk neat and tidy at the end of the day. Have consideration of the night cleaners—don't throw food and liquid in your wastebasket.

Take good care of your own plants or flowers.

Be meticulous about your use of the office rest room.

Don't make personal telephone calls in the office. If you have to make one, keep it short. No chitchat. It demoralizes everyone within earshot.

Don't use your office as a grooming center. Take care of makeup-applying, hair-combing, and nail-trimming in the rest room.

Don't chew gum in the office. A face contorted with fast chewing detracts from the office landscape—and from what others think of you.

Don't eat food at your desk.

Don't drop by someone's desk to chat just because you're not busy. The other person may need to concentrate at that particular moment. Besides, you should utilize any free time to educate yourself about the company's operations.

Don't read magazines or newspapers at your desk when you're not busy, either. It creates a sloppy, lazy impression.

Don't clutter your desk with family snapshots and memorabilia. You may love your dog more than anyone else in the world, but his picture doesn't belong on your desk!

Never lean back in your chair and put your feet on the desk. The sight of the soles of your feet does not inspire anyone.

Don't take sides in office gossip and office politics. Stay out of any back-stabbing operations. Your friend today may become your enemy tomorrow, if you participate in any maliciousness.

Be "up front" at all times with everyone. If you are honest, friendly, and cheerful, you'll find that things will go well for you.

Business Entertaining

When an office colleague invites me to have lunch, I don't have any problems regarding the check. We both pay it—equally. But when I'm with a client and he or she suggests we continue our discussion over lunch, I never know what to do.

If it's a client who contributes to your firm's profits, you should take him or her to lunch. If it's a source from whom you buy, let the person take you to lunch, but make it a modest one.

It's important never to feel indebted to anyone just because of lunch.

If you want to pick someone's brain at lunch and gain some good advice, the lunch should be on you.

If you deal with someone who is always making you pick up the check, and you feel it's unfair, transact your next business in the office, not around lunchtime!

As a woman executive, I deal with many conservative older men in the financial community who are very uncomfortable about my picking up the lunch check. How can I put them at ease?

You can always arrange with the restaurant, if they know you well, to simply send you the bill the next day. Or you can pass by the captain's desk at dessert time, when your lunch companion thinks you have gone to make a telephone call, and settle your bill then. Most men who feel very uncom-

fortable having a woman take them to lunch the first time
feel better by the third time, and by the fourth time in their
lives it happens, they don't even think about it.

What are the components of a well-designed business invitation?

Good stock; a sense of dignity; efficient communication:
in other words, relate exactly *who* is giving the party, *what
kind* of party it is, *when* it is, and *at what time* it is, *where* it
is, and *what the occasion is,* and *how to RSVP.*

If spouses and guests are invited, that should be communicated; if the party is held in an out-of-the-way place, a
map should be included, or parking directions should be
given. If special dress requirements are in order, that should
be stated on the invitation, too.

Here's a sample invitation:

COMPANY LOGO

Mr. Eugene Brown, Chairman
Ms. Melanie Adams, President
of the Dutchess County Metalworks Corporation
request the pleasure of the company of
Mr. Ralph Gordon and guest
at a dinner
commemorating the company's Fiftieth Anniversary
and honoring the employees who have been with the
company for all those fifty years
on Friday, June third
at seven o'clock
Bloomington Country Club
River Road
Poughkeepsie

RSVP
Office of the Chairman
(000) 000-0000
13 Seacrest Road
Kingston, New York zip

On the inside of this double-fold invitation, the following is printed:

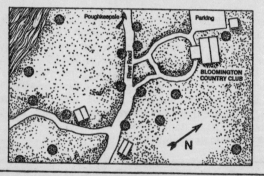

> The Honorable John H. Harding
> Governor of the State of New York
> will make the opening remarks promptly at 7:30 P.M.

This invitation includes all the necessary information. There is obviously no parking problem at a country club, but the problem of how to find it is solved with the map on the inside page. The fact that the governor is making "opening remarks" promptly at 7:30 means he obviously can't stay for dinner, so if one wants to hear his speech, one had better be there on time.

When people respond to this invitation, the single people, like Ralph Gordon, must furnish the names of their dates. Here would be his proper written RSVP to the chairman's office:

Mr. Ralph Gordon and Ms. Stephanie Wright accept with pleasure the kind invitation of Mr. Eugene Brown and Ms. Melanie Adams to dinner on Friday, June third.

(Ralph Gordon can also telephone his RSVP to the chairman's secretary; the written response is, however, much nicer.)

How would my company print a program for an affair like the Dutchess County Metalworks anniversary dinner?

You might have the company logo printed or embossed on the outside of the four-page booklet. Inside, as you open to two pages, the left side would contain the menu, and the right side the program. For example:

Left side:

MENU

Salmon à la Russe

Noisettes of Veal
Fresh Asparagus Hollandaise
Broiled Tomatoes
Salad Mimosa

Pommes Charlotte Dutchess County
Demitasse

Callaway Chenin Blanc
Korbel Champagne

Right side:

PROGRAM

Opening remarks by The Honorable John H. Harding
Governor of the State of New York

Welcoming remarks by Mr. Eugene Brown

Introduction of the Board of Directors
Ms. Melanie Adams

Presentation to the Fifty-Year Employees
Mr. Anthony Caldwell, for the Board of
Directors

"Predictions for Fifty Years from Now"
A Musical Presentation by the Fifty-Year Employees

Dance Music by Lester Lanin and His Orchestra

What are the various ways in which a business invitation may be issued?

An invitation may be extended by telephone, by a letter signed by a member of management, by a Mailgram (when time is short), by engraved invitation (when it's a very special occasion,) or by printed invitation.

If your company telephones its invitations, be sure to follow up—if time permits—with a written reminder, so that recipients won't make mistakes as to the date, time, etc., of your invitation.

RSVP cards sent with self-addressed envelopes are proper, aren't they?

Yes, it's too bad that we have to resort to this shortcut, but people are so irresponsible about responding to invitations that the fill-in card ("Put a check here if you're coming") has become a necessity.

I handle my boss's invitations. What is the proper acceptance for an invitation?

Ms. Jane Fairchild Stark
accepts with pleasure
the kind invitatoin of Mr. John Lance
for lunch on Wednesday, June first.

(Write today's date here)

What if one's boss can't accept because he's away?

Send his regret in a form of letter to be signed by you:

Dear Mr. Lance:

I am taking the liberty of regretting your kind invitation to Ms. Jane Fairchild Stark for lunch on June 1. Ms. Stark is in the Far East and won't return until June 5. I know how very much she will regret missing your luncheon, and on her behalf I thank you for inviting her.

Sincerely,
Susan Smith

Are you supposed to treat a business event like a social one? Send a thank-you note?

Absolutely. A business event calls for good manners every bit as much as a private social affair. A lot of planning, time, and someone's money have gone into it, so thanks are in order. Even if you're invited to lunch in a restaurant, you should send a thank-you note within two or three days of the engagement.

May a business thank-you note be typed?

A business thank-you note *should* be typed.

When does a business party call for a receiving line, and who stands in it?

When there's a big crowd, and many people do not know their hosts, a receiving line is called for. The number of people who stand in it should be minimal. If it's a party like the one given for the fiftieth-anniversary given by the chairman and president of the Dutchess County Metalworks Corporation, the receiving line would consist only of the chairman and the president of the company. The governor should be invited to stand in the line, too—he doesn't have to if he doesn't wish to. Their spouses would not stand in the receiving line.

Are badges a good thing to have for big receptions? If so, how is the name recorded, and where is the best place to wear a badge?

Badges are an excellent idea for big parties, to help people make introductions, to help people remember names, and to help people learn who works for whom.

The name should be recorded without a title, unless a person is a doctor, judge, congressman, ambassador, clergyman, or someone who needs his or her title known to others.

If John Smith is just "Mr.," his badge would read "John Smith." But if his career carries a title, he would be "Ambassador Smith," "Dr. John Smith," etc.

The company name should be put under the person's name. If the person is a member of top management, his or her title should be included on the badge. If a cocktail guest at a reception for two thousand is chatting with one of her hosts, she ought to know if that person is the chairman of the board!

Is it absolutely necessary to involve one's spouse in evening business entertaining?

Not in today's world of dual careers, particularly if there are young children left at home. It is much better if one parent stays home with those young children than to have to go out with his or her spouse and then have to attend his or her own company's functions in the evening, too.

If it's a very important company dinner, of course, the person should indicate that it means a lot to have the spouse attend.

If you're entertaining people from the outside in the executive dining room, are you supposed to use place cards?

By all means, use them for any group of eight or more.

Does seating matter in the executive dining room?

Yes, protocol should be observed in every case where foreign and visiting business people or officials come to lunch. The most-important guest sits on the host's right, the second-most-important guest on the host's left. The second-most-important host should sit opposite the host, the third- and fourth-most-important guest would sit on his or her right and left.

Telephone Manners

What is the definition of a good telephone voice in an office?

A voice that is warm, friendly, businesslike, and efficient.

How should an office telephone be answered?

That depends on what kind of business the office handles. The secretary-nurse to a cancer surgeon must handle his or her calls differently from the secretary to a used-car dealer. The secretary should understand the nature of the business and the image of the company or of the boss that should be relayed to the public. It is therefore important for the boss to communicate that message before a telephone is even picked up by a new employee in that office.

If I want to be efficient in handling telephone calls, what do I do?

Let's say you are calling a person and the secretary has never heard of you.

"Mr. Nelson's office."

"This is Jane Durham calling. May I please speak to Mr. Nelson?"

"From what company, please?"

"I am the vice-president of Gordon Sales, Incorporated. Mr. Nelson's colleague on the board of the Lighthouse for the Blind suggested that I call him."

"Oh, I see. This is Lighthouse for the Blind business."

"Yes."

"Just a minute, please, I'll see if I can put you through to Mr. Nelson."

Isn't it demeaning when you're trying to speak to someone to have to explain to the secretary exactly why you're calling?

It's not demeaning at all. It's just good business. If you can get across to the secretary how important your business is, she'll be able to influence her boss to call you back.

What should an executive say when he's answering his own telephone?

Whether he or she *always* answers his or her own phone, or whether it's an exceptional case, the executive should answer with the name. "David Jones speaking" or "Marian McNamara speaking" is all that is necessary.

But what if you are on the line with a pest who just won't let you go and who keeps insisting? Is it all right just to hang up?

Not abruptly. No, be gentle, and polite. One never knows the circumstances. Just interrupt the caller with an apology: "I'm sorry, our tieline to our Alaska office is ringing. I must pick up. Please write me what you have to say." Then you can hang up!

Don't you think it's rude when you go to someone's office for a preset appointment and that person is constantly interrupted by telephone calls?

Absolutely. Only the most urgent calls should be put through when an appointment is in progress.

Isn't it also rude to be talking on the telephone and to be talking to someone in your office at the same time?

Very. It's a slap in the face to the person who is calling you, even though you don't mean it to be. When you are actually on the line, you should be attentive (and not chewing or eating, either!).

How do you feel about businesses that use answering machines?

Many small or new businesses have to rely on the answering machines as an economy measure. As soon as the business can afford it, however, an answering service or, even better, a receptionist or secretary is important, in order to polish the image of professional competence.

Isn't it all right to make a business call to someone's home?

No, unless it is a matter of utmost emergency. The average person is extremely put off by a business call interrupting his or her few moments of relaxation at home.

If you do have to call someone at home, apologize heartily to the person and to the person's spouse for the unwelcome interruption even before you begin your message.

We have a good answering service that operates when my associate, our secretary, and I are out of the office. I never see those people and I don't quite know how to acknowledge the good job they are doing for us. Do we tip them?

No, don't tip them, but send them a big box of candy, fruit, or a fruitcake during the holidays. Tell them over the telephone that they're doing a great job, and once a year, write their supervisor or the head of the service and tell him or her how wonderful they are. You'll see, your service will get better and better!

What's the secret of having a good relationship with your answering service? Mine is slipshod and careless.

A telephone-answering service is usually only as good as your instructions are. Communicate very carefully (on paper, so it's on the record) exactly how you want the service to operate, what is to be said, what excuses are to be made, etc.

If the service persists in being inefficient, transfer to another.

Office Gifts

I am secretary to a very nice woman executive. Am I supposed to give her a present at Christmas? I would like to, but I want to do the proper thing.

The only kind of gift you should give is one that is not expensive, and one that is not personal. For example, if you know she needs a new pen or a new small agenda to keep in her briefcase, that's the kind of gift for you to give her.

Should I give presents to my immediate staff when they get married, have babies, and invite me to everything in their families from their daughter's graduation from college to their son's bar mitzvah? I somehow feel the formal invitation requires a present "from the boss."

A boss could go broke giving gifts for everything that happens in his close personal staff's lives. Keep your gift giving to Christmastime (bonuses are the best), and write a good letter of congratulation to the person involved in your staff members' invitations. One of the greatest letters I ever saw was from the chairman of the board of a corporation, sent in response to a christening invitation from his receptionist. The letter was addressed to the baby, and its two short paragraphs of clever text were worth far more to the parents than any sterling-silver present.

How can I gracefully solve the problem of our traditional office Christmas party? It has gotten out of hand. Everyone drinks too much and makes fools of themselves.

Very simply. Just don't have the usual office party. Give everyone tickets to the local symphony concert instead. Or give an amusing breakfast party, where liquor is not even served.

Business Travel

Is it all right for men and women traveling on business for their company to share a suite?

It's better for the firm's good name if the sexes are kept separate—even though nothing but business may be transacted in that suite!

I'm an executive secretary, and when I travel with my boss, he often dictates to me in the morning in his room, still dressed in his pajamas. I feel uneasy about this but don't know how to handle it.

The next time he receives you in his pajamas, tell him you are going back to your room, and to please call you when he is dressed "and ready to give dictation." Do it with a smile. He'll understand.

I will be taking my secretary with me to Europe. Am I supposed to pay all her expenses as we go along?

She should be given her own advance and pay all her own expenses, even her hotel bills. If she's expert at keeping records, perhaps she should pay *your* expenses, so they are properly documented!

If a man and woman are traveling together on business, should they split absolutely everything, right down to the last dime? Something like a bottle of wine ordered at dinner, for example?

Only one person should assume the cost of the wine. You should be careful about splitting the charges on almost everything, however. Keep good records in your book, and if necessary, you can reimburse your travel companion upon your return to headquarters.

It may be lonely for a salesman who's always on the road, but for a woman who travels on business alone, it's worse. She doesn't have the freedom a man does. Is there something to help fortify her spirit and to lessen her sensitivity about being a woman alone?

There is no reason for a woman to sequester herself in her hotel room for cocktails and dinner with the TV set if she would rather have a drink in the bar and dinner in one of the downstairs restaurants.

She can carry her "security blanket" with her to the bar. The security blanket may consist of business folders or her briefcase, conspicuous signs of a woman at work.

No one could possibly accuse her of being a "pickup" if she comes into the bar with her work, orders a drink, glances at a file or two, and then sits back to relax and enjoy her cocktail.

Is it all right for her to accept invitations to dinner, then?

If it's someone who wants to join her for dinner right there in the hotel, there is no danger. She should pay for her own drinks and her own meal.

If she goes out after dinner to local bars with a stranger, she is asking for trouble.

I never know what to do about the hotel maid. Am I supposed to tip her?

Yes. Leave one dollar per night in an average hostelry. If you're in a luxury hotel, leave her two dollars for every night you spend there. Hotel management generally does not compensate the cleaning people generously, and those tips mean a lot.

Correspondence: Our Stationery, the Names We Call Ourselves, the Letters We Write

Stationery and the Name You Use for Yourself

As a wedding present, I'm receiving engraved stationery. What kind should I get, and how should my monogram be done?

Choose either single-sheet notepaper or the double-fold kind. (The latter can be used for writing invitations, too.) For your monogram, you can use either your new married-last-name letter, or your given-name and new married-last-name letters, or your given and family names combined with your married name. If you are retaining your maiden name in marriage, you would use your given and family names. In other words, if your name is Anne Golden, and you're marrying John Miller, you could use any of these: M, AGM, AM, or, if you're retaining your maiden name, AG.

I can't afford engraved stationery. Is it wrong to send notes on printed paper? Invitations, too?

No, it's perfectly right and proper to use printed paper.

When you're having stationery printed, it's traditional to put the return address on the back flap, isn't it?

Traditional, yes, but not a good idea today. The post office wants return addresses on the upper-left-hand portion of the front side of the envelope, so it's easier to return to the sender.

I want to have stationery printed that has my telephone number, full married name, and address on it, so I can use it for personal business. How should it be laid out?

Here is one way of doing it: Put your married name at the top center of the page, with the address, city, and zip code right beneath. Place the area code and telephone number at the top right.

What about engraved cards? One doesn't see them much anymore.

Most people use business cards; not so many have engraved calling cards made anymore. Those who do, use them mostly for gift-enclosure cards. The traditional engraved card for a married woman would be "Mrs. Robert Smith"; sometimes both husband's and wife's names are on the card: "Mr. and Mrs. Robert Smith." There just isn't that much use for them anymore.

What is being used a great deal are "correspondence cards"—rectangular cards of a heavy stock, more or less shaped like a postcard or smaller, with a person's name or monogram at the top left or at top center. The envelopes, of course, are matching.

I thought you couldn't use colored stationery in formal social matters.

You can use colored stationery today, with contrasting colored border, printing or engraving for everything except writing condolence notes. The latter should be written on white, cream-colored, or pale gray stationery. The engraving for very formal notepaper can be any dark color (black, maroon, navy, brown, etc.).

What kind of personal stationery should a man have?

A large single sheet of white, gray, cream, or tan is best, with his full name printed or engraved at top center. He can either include his office address beneath his name, or his home address, or neither.

A man in the fashion or design business usually has other kinds of stationery, with unusual color combinations and shapes—this kind would be inappropriate for someone in the conservative business world.

Letter Forms and Signatures

When you don't know whether the person who will get your letter is male or female, which is preferable, to say "Dear Sir," "Dear Sirs," "Dear Madam," "Ladies and Gentlemen," or what?

Write a memo rather than a letter. Then there is no reference to the gender of the person who opens and copes with your letter, nor is there any need for a closing salutation. You might use the following form:

Your address
City, state and zip code
The date

MEMO FOR: Name of the company here
Address of the company (include department, if known)
City, state, and zip code

RE: State Here Your Business (for example: *Discrepancy in My August Bill;* or *Merchandise That Has Not Arrived;* or *Your Letter of June 18th;* or whatever the reason is for writing the memo).

Start the body of the memo here.

Put your name here

If I'm married but need to communicate both my husband's and my maiden names, how do I do it in a personal letter?

Very simply. Either sign your letter "Jennifer Smith" and type "Mrs. George A." in parentheses beneath the "Jennifer Smith," or have your personal business stationery printed with your married name at top; then you only have to sign "Jennifer Smith" at the bottom of the communication.

How should women be listed when their names are on a club roster, for example, or given to a newspaper for publicity on the officers of a club or on the chairmen and committee members for a benefit?

Since the advent of the women's movement, some women now insist on a special listing of their names—a "Ms." before the name, for example. Some women use their maiden names, others want to use their husband's names. What results is a hodgepodge of "Mrs.," "Miss," "Ms.," maiden names, husband's names, etc. The best way to uniformly and fairly present a list of alphabetized women's names is as follows (note that there are no titles, except when it's pertinent, such as in the case of a doctor):

> Anderson, Anna (Mrs. Lars J.)
> Ayers, Susan
> Baldwin, Mary Lee (Mrs. George W.)
> Bryers, Dr. Dorothy J.
> Chase, Lyn (Mrs. Theodore A.)
> Doughty, Janet

I firmly believe our society must move forward in the use of women's first names. It's a feminist viewpoint, but it also makes for efficiency and saves everyone else a lot of time and trouble.

How should a divorcée be listed—by her family name and her former husband's last name?

No, that's old-fashioned. In the "old days," if Barbara Woodson married Neil Crawford and then divorced him, she would be known the rest of her life, unless she remarried, as "Mrs. Woodson Crawford." That's confusing and useless. Today she is "Mrs. Barbara Crawford."

Are a lot of divorced women resuming their maiden names?

Yes, particularly when the children are grown up and "out of the nest." A woman often kept her former husband's last name because it was the same as the children's. When the children are off on their own, it no longer seems important.

When does a "Jr." drop the suffix?

When his father dies. If both the late father and the son are well known, however, the son keeps the "Jr." to avoid confusion. (A case in point: Franklin Roosevelt, Jr.)

If you have the suffix "III" or "IV" after your name, when do you drop it?

Whenever you feel tired of using it, or if you feel that others think it's a snobbish affectation for you to use it.

How do you address an invitation to a couple when she has retained her maiden name?

Their names go on one line, his first, as in the English tradition:

Mr. Jerome Weston and Ms. (or Miss) Marianne Nelson
Address
City, state, and zip code

Is it "Esq." or "Esquire," and do women lawyers have the right to use it in conjunction with their names?

"Esquire" came to us from England, where it indicated a knight's eldest son and bearer of the hereditary title. Today some lawyers use "Esq." (abbreviated) following their names, and never combined with "Mr." or "Mrs." Women lawyers certainly do have the right to use it. In extremely formal correspondence or diplomatic letters, "Esquire" is written out and not abbreviated.

My lawyer is a doctor of jurisprudence and likes to use it in her correspondence. Why isn't she both "Esq." and "J.D." after her name?

The "J.D." following her name (just as an "M.D." following a doctor's name) is considered sufficient. Some lawyers who have the right to use "J.D." will not use it.

How do you know whether to write "Dear Mrs. Jones" or "Dear Mary"? I don't want to be too familiar, yet I never seem to know when I've progressed to the first-name basis in correspondence.

If your correspondent calls you by your first name, you have no problem. You reciprocate. If you haven't received correspondence from the other person, here's how to judge the proper name to use: If you know the person quite well, write "Dear Mary." If she is an older person or someone who commands respect, like your clergyman's wife or an associate professor, write "Dear Mrs. Jones." If you have met her once or twice and feel a kindred relationship, yet you don't know her well enough to write "Dear Mary," address her like this: "Dear Mary Jones." When she responds by mail and you have to write to her again, you can drop the "Jones."

Unmarried People Who Must Be Treated as Couples

How do I introduce two people who are living together but are not married?

Just introduce them by their separate names. If people at your party ask if they are married or engaged, answer "They are living together." It is another form of status quo: married, divorced, engaged, and now "living together."

What should I call the man with whom I am living? I can't call him "my lover" in polite society. Can I use the term "My live-together"? "My apartment mate"?

There are a hundred terms used, each one more "cute" than the next. The most straightforward term takes a little longer to write or say but it's a lot more dignified: "the person with whom I live."

We want to have stationery printed with our two names and our common address. Is this good form?

It is much better form for each to have his or her own stationery, and then for either of you to write the letter, mentioning the other in the body of the letter. For example, Madeline Gunlock would write a letter thanking her hosts for the weekend visit: "Gregory and I had the most wonderful time, and he asked me to relay his sincere thanks to you both for everything you did to make the weekend so great!"

Do you have to send separate invitations to two people who are not married but living together?

No. They receive one invitation. Their names are on separate lines (not on one line, like a married couple), and they are listed alphabetically. For example:

> Ms. Madeline Gunlock
> Mr. Gregory Williams
> Address

How do you address invitations to a homosexual pair?

You send them one, and you list their names alphabetically, on separate lines, following the same rule that applies to unmarried couples.

Is it all right to invite one member of the homosexual couple without the other if you don't know the other member or if you don't like the other member?

No, it's very rude and ungracious to invite one without the other. A business lunch is one thing—one can be invited without offending the other—but a social engagement in the evening or on the weekend is another thing. They must be invited together if they are living together in an open relationship.

Doesn't inviting unmarried people who live together and homosexuals who live together as couples signify moral acceptance of the arrangement?

No. How one feels personally about their relationships is entirely another matter. We are talking here about interaction between human beings in a kind and gracious way, not about morals and mores.

Layout and Composition of Letters

What is the correct form for laying out a social letter?

If your address is not printed on the top of your stationery, you should write (or type) it at the upper right, with the date beneath. This is the proper form:

> Address
> City, state and zip
> Today's date

(Skip some spaces here, and leave wide margins all around the page)

Dear Amy,

Begin the body of your letter here. It's nice to say something about Amy's own life, such as "I hope you have had a good summer," or "I hope the news on Jim is good." Then get on with what you have to say.

When you have finished the letter, jump some more spaces, and write your closing salutation.

> Much love (or Sincerely),
> Sign your given name

If you're writing someone a note on your informals (folded notepaper), what sequence do you follow in writing on the pages?

If you have a monogram on the top side, begin inside on the bottom half of the paper. (If you have a very long letter, begin on the top half of the inside fold.) Continue on the backside half of the notepaper. If there is no monogram on the top side, begin writing your note there, on the front.

Please give me some examples of when you would use your good notepaper.

For one thing, you would accept or regret invitations on your good notepaper. You would also write thank-you notes for parties you've attended, gifts you've received, favors that have been done for you.

You also write a note to a relative or a friend when something good happens to that person; also when something sad happens to him or her.

You would write to convey important information.

Below are some sample "main-bodies-of-the-text" letters showing when and how they are written:

... You can't imagine how much we're enjoying the big crock of cheddar. The family fights for it constantly, so I have to hide it from them all. There's never been a holiday present so eagerly received by the whole family! ...

... It was the best weekend I've had all summer, and you arranged so many wonderful things. It was relaxing and amusing, and I loved meeting all your friends. Even the weather cooperated to make it a fantastic experience. Thank you *so* much for having me! ...

... We both appreciate so much what you did for Grace. Your recommendation, the wonderful letter you wrote on her behalf, cinched her getting the job, I'm sure. We will never be able to thank you enough. ...

... I just heard. Billy made the team! Congratulations to all of you. I'm sure this is one season you won't miss a home game. He must be in seventh heaven. We can all relax now, knowing that State will win all its games. . . .

. . . We just heard the bad news. It's impossible to come up with some good pat phrases at a time like this. One can't put into words what one feels. But just remember this, we're all here, ready to help, ready to do anything you ask of us. You're on our minds and in our hearts and prayers every second of the time. . . .

How do you write a good letter of social reference for a friend going to live in another city?

Give the background of the person who's moving to the other person's city in some detail. Don't pressure your friends (to whom the letter is addressed) into immediate action. Write something like, "If you and Sue ever have friends in for drinks, we'd really appreciate your having the Turners. It would mean a lot to them to meet you and some of your friends."

How do you write a good fund-raising letter?

For one thing, save any letters *you* receive that you found compelling and persuasive. Copy their good points.

Make your letter short and to the point. Send supporting materials to describe what the nonprofit institution does. Explain how much has to be raised by such-and-such a date. Give a clear description of what the money is to be used for. Don't "suggest" that your friend give a specific amount of money. Rather describe what a gift of $1,000 will do, what a gift of $100 will do, and what a donation of $10 will do.

What makes an effective letter of complaint? Like telling the neighbors their barking dog keeps us awake all night?

State your case firmly, clearly, without emotion, and without threats. Document the number of nights, the number of hours the dog barked, and the number of people in your home being kept awake. "Suggest" that immediate action be taken by the owner, and close on a nice, polite note, such as: "I'm sure you have not been aware of our discomfort; it is really my fault for not having brought it to your attention sooner."

A polite letter of complaint makes the recipient feel somewhat guilty. A nasty one makes him or her feel hostile, and things could get a lot worse before they get better.

Greeting Cards

When do you send a personal note, and when do you send a greeting card?

That's a matter of personal preference. If you're accepting or regretting an invitation, that should be done on your own stationery. But for most other events or reasons for communicating with another person, greeting cards are fine. What *is* important is the personalization of every greeting card you send.

For example, inside a graduation greeting card, you might write something about your hopes for that graduate's "brilliant and happy future." In a condolence card you should write a message about your happy memories of the person who has died, and of your offer to help the family in any way. A valentine is a hundred times more effective if you write a little message on it, like "This only says *half* of it!" In other words, write something in your own manner, to reinforce and personalize what is expressed on the card.

As for the really obscene, vulgar cards—they are only for obscene, vulgar people to send.

Should Christmas cards have one's name printed on them, or should one sign each one personally and forget the printing?

It's a good idea to have your name printed on them. Then the recipient will definitely know who sent the cards (each year there are several cards received in our household which remain anonymous—we don't have a clue who sent them!).

However, it's nice to put a diagonal slash through the printed name and to write a little message to each recipient. It can be a short letter, full of family news, or it can be a phrase as short as this: "Hope the Reynoldses have a great New Year!" It adds a personal touch.

Is it all right to send Christmas cards to Jews?

Some Jews are sensitive about receiving cards with the word "Christ" involved in any way. It is better for a Christian to send Jewish friends "Holiday Greetings" or "Happy New Year" cards.

If you're sending business Christmas cards, do you send them to a couple, if you know your friend is married?

If you have not met the spouse of the business person to whom you are sending a card, send it only to your business friend. You might mention inside the card something like, "I hope all of you have a wonderful holiday season," or something that would include a family, if there happens to be one.

Protocol

When you're introducing your parents, relatives, friends, teachers, clergyman—I never know who should be introduced to whom.

Just remember: the youngest and the least important is introduced to the older and the more important. Often, someone who may be very important in one's life is relegated to a lesser position, as a common courtesy. For example, if you and your parents meet one of your graduate-school professors on the street, you give the courtesy to your teacher, even though your parents may be the most important people in your life! "Professor Harris, I'd like to introduce my parents to you, Mr. and Mrs. Williamson. Mom and Dad, this is Professor Gerald Harris—you've heard me speak about him often."

If you're planning a top-level function at a hotel, and there'll be several high-placed government officials present, how do you seat them at the table?

Here's an abbreviated unofficial list of high-ranking officials, showing their place in the order of things:

The President of the United States; the Vice-President; the Speaker of the House of Representatives; the Chief Justice; former Presidents; the Secretary of State; Secretary General of the United Nations; Ambassadors of Foreign Powers; Widows of former Presidents of the United States; Associate Justices of the Supreme Court of the United States; the Cabinet, in this order:

Secretary of the Treasury
Defense
Attorney General
Interior
Agriculture
Commerce
Labor
Health and Human Services
Housing and Urban Development
Transportation
Energy
Education

The United States Representative to the United Nations; Director, Office of Management and Budget; Chairman, Council of Economic Advisers; Special Representative for Trade Negotiations; the Senate; Governors of the States; former Vice-Presidents of the United States; the House of Representatives; Assistants to the President; Chargés d'Affaires of Foreign Powers; the Undersecretaries of the Executive Departments and the Deputy Secretaries; Administrator, Agency for International Development; Director, U.S. Arms Control and Disarmament Agency; Secretaries of the Army, Navy, and Air Force; Chairman, Board of Governors of the Federal Reserve System; Chairman, Council on Environmental Quality; Chairman, Joint Chiefs of Staff; Chiefs of Staff of the Army, Navy, and Air Force (ranked according to date of appointment); Commandant of the Marine Corps; five-star Generals of the Army and Fleet Admirals; Secretary General, Organization of American States. *Et ceteral*

Hypothetical Questions

How would you write to the President and First Lady in Washington?

You wouldn't. You would write to one or the other:

> The President
> The White House
> 1600 Pennsylvania Avenue
> Washington, D.C. 20500

or you would write to:

> "Mrs. Jones" (if they were named Jones)
> The White House
> (Same address as above)

As your salutation for the President, you would write: "Dear Mr. President" (one never uses his last name in a letter).

Her salutation would read: "Dear Mrs. Jones" (her given name is never used).

If, however, you were going to send an invitation to them both, you would write on the envelope:

> The President and Mrs. Jones
> The White House, etc.

What about a former President? Is he still called President?

If you're writing him a letter, you would address it: "The Honorable Anson Jones" (and "Mrs. Jones," if she's being invited to something with her husband).

You would address him as "Mr. President" or "Sir" or "Mr. Jones."

You would introduce him as "Former President Jones"

or as "The Honorable Anson Jones, former President of the United States."

How would I send an invitation to the Chief Justice and his wife?

You would address it: "The Chief Justice and Mrs. Springs." Use their home address.

My old friend Mrs. William Dutton is now a cabinet officer. Do I write to her as "Mrs. William Dutton"?

No, if you're writing her a business letter at her office, address it like this:

> The Honorable
> Jennifer Dutton
> The Attorney General of the United States
> The Department of Justice
> Washington, D.C. 20530

The salutation on the letter would be: "Dear Madam Attorney General."

If you're sending her and her husband a social invitation, write it to:

> The Honorable
> The Attorney General
>   and Mr. Dutton
> Home address

When someone's a senator or congressman, do you write to "Senator and Mrs." or what?

If you're writing him at the office, address the envelope like this:

> The Honorable
> Andrew V. Updike
> United States Senate
> Senate Office Building
> Washington, D.C. 20510

The salutation would be: "Dear Senator Updike."
If you're sending the couple an invitation, address it:

> The Honorable
> Andrew V. Updike
>   and Mrs. Updike
> Home address

For a congressman, you would put "The Honorable" and
then the name beneath. For the salutation you would put
"Dear Ms. Pratt" instead of "Congressman Pratt."

How do you introduce senators and congressmen?

You give their title, name, and state. For example: "Senator Mills from New Mexico" ... "Representative Marcello from Massachusetts."

Does the same apply to a governor?

Yes, he's introduced as "Governor Hardwick of Iowa."
He's written to as:

> The Honorable
> Jeremy B. Hardwick
> Governor of Iowa
> State Capitol, etc.

He and his wife would be sent an invitation as: "The
Governor and Mrs. Hardwick" (or if it's a female governor,
"The Governor and Mr. Bell").

How do you tell Army military rank?

In order of rank, Army-officer personnel are as follows:

General of the Army	five silver stars
General	four silver stars
Lieutenant General	three silver stars
Major General	two silver stars
Brigadier General	one silver star
Colonel	silver eagle

Lieutenant Colonel	silver oak leaf
Major	gold oak leaf
Captain	two silver bars
First Lieutenant	one silver bar
Second Lieutenant	one gold bar
Chief Warrant Officer	one gold bar, brown enamel top, gold longitudinal center
Warrant Officer, Junior Grade	same as above, except gold center is latitudinal

What are the symbols of Navy rank?

Rank is indicated on blue uniforms by gold stripes on the sleeves, and on white or dress khaki uniforms on the detachable shoulder boards.

Here is the order of officer personnel of the Navy by rank:

FLEET ADMIRAL—five silver stars, one 2″ stripe, and four ½″ sleeve stripes, with star of line officer

ADMIRAL—four silver stars, one 2″ stripe, and three ½″ sleeve stripes, with star of line officer or corps device

VICE-ADMIRAL—three silver stars, one 2″ stripe, and two ½″ sleeve stripes, star of line officer or corps device

REAR-ADMIRAL—two silver stars, one 2″ stripe, and one ½″ sleeve stripe, star of line officer or corps device

COMMODORE—one silver star, one 2″ sleeve stripe, star of line officer or corps device

CAPTAIN—silver spread eagle, four ½″ stripes, star of line officer or corps device

COMMANDER—silver oak leaf, three ½″ stripes, star of line officer or corps device

LIEUTENANT COMMANDER—gold oak leaf, two ½″ stripes with ¼″ one between, star of line officer or corps device

LIEUTENANT—two silver bars, two ½″ stripes, star of line officer or corps device

LIEUTENANT, JUNIOR GRADE—one silver bar, one ½″ stripe with ¼″ one above, star of line officer or corps device

ENSIGN—one gold bar, one ½" gold stripe, star of line
  officer or corps device
CHIEF WARRANT OFFICER—one ¼" broken gold stripe
  and specialty device
WARRANT OFFICER—one ¼" broken gold stripe and
  specialty device

What about the Marine Corps, Air Force, and Coast Guard?

The rank and insignia of the Marine Corps and the Air
Force are the same as the Army. The Coast Guard is the
same as the Navy.

If you have a military couple with the wife outranking her husband, how are they addressed in an invitation?

If she outranks her husband, her name comes first on invitations; she is introduced before him, too.
  On an envelope:

> Major General Alice Jenkins and Brigadier
>   General James Jenkins
> U.S. Air Force
> Office address

They would be introduced as: "Major General Jenkins and
Brigadier General Jenkins."

What do you call chaplains in the armed forces?

They are called by their military rank, both officially and
socially. Informally, however, they are addressed as "Chap-
lain," "Father," or "Rabbi."

Do people who are reserve officers or National Guard officers not on active duty use their titles?

No. However, career military who are retired retain their
military titles, unless they are involved in something like an
official situation abroad, where people might think they are
still active and carrying out the orders of the U.S. government.

What is the protocol with female students at military academies?

A woman at the United States Military Academy is called "Cadet Mary Smith," just as a male student is called "Cadet William Scribner." A woman at Annapolis or at the United States Merchant Marine Academy is "Midshipman Ann Schultz." One writes a letter to her as "Dear Cadet Smith" or "Dear Midshipman Schultz."

How do you write a letter to a rabbi?

If the rabbi holds a scholastic degree, it's addressed to:

> Rabbi Jerome Sachs, D.D., LL.D.
> Temple Emmanuel
> Address

You would write the letter "Dear Rabbi Sachs," or "Dear Dr. Sachs," which is a matter of the rabbi's personal preference.

A rabbi without a scholastic degree is always addressed by the title and by the family name.

How do you address a Protestant clergyman with a doctor's degree?

You would write "The Reverend John S. Baines, D.D.," followed by the address. You would send an invitation to him and his wife in this manner: "The Reverend Dr. and Mrs. John S. Baines," followed by an address. If it's a woman who's the clergyman with the degree, it would be: "The Reverend Dr. Felicia Warren and Mr. Robert Warren."

What about a clergyman without a degree?

Use this for the address: "The Reverend Daniel Davison," and for an invitation to the couple, "The Reverend and Mrs. Daniel Davison."

How do you address a bishop of the Mormon church?

"Bishop" is used only within the organization during his term of office. Otherwise he is:

Mr. John Ellinghouse
Church of Jesus Christ of Latter-Day Saints
Address

He is addressed as "Mr. Ellinghouse" in correspondence.

If I want to write a letter to the pope in Rome, how do I address it?

It's highly unlikely he'll receive it—it's far better to send it to the North American College in Rome. However, if you want to write him, send it to:

His Holiness, the Pope
Vatican City
00187 Rome, Italy

If you have the good fortune to meet him, you address him as "Your Holiness" or "Most Holy Father."

There's a protocol regarding writing to cardinals of the Catholic Church, isn't there?

Yes. One puts the title "Cardinal" in between his first and last names. He is always addressed as "Your Eminence" and referred to as "His Eminence." You would write to him like this:

His Eminence, Joseph
Cardinal Matthews
Archbishop of Boston
Address

How about writing to a priest?

If he's a monsignor, you write to him as:

The Right Reverend Monsignor Patrick Callahan
St. Monica's Church, etc.

You would use "Dear Monsignor Callahan" in the salutation.

If he's a priest, you would put on the envelope:

> The Reverend Father James J. Harding
> Church of St. Thomas More, etc.

He would be introduced and saluted as "Father Harding," although friends who are close to him might call him "Father Jim."

How is a nun addressed?

If you know the nun's order, you write the initials after her name:

> Sister Anne Creed, RSCJ
> Convent of the Sacred Heart
> Address

She is called "Sister Creed."

How does one write to the Queen of England, her husband, and Prince Charles?

The proper form is to write to their private secretaries, not to them. However, if you were a head of state writing to the Queen, you would write:

> Her Majesty,
> Queen Elizabeth II
> Buckingham Palace
> London SW1A 1AA
> England

In talking to her you would say, "Your Majesty," and then, later on, you would call her "ma'am."

For her husband, you would write:

> His Royal Highness,
> The Prince Philip, Duke of Edinburgh
> Buckingham Palace, etc.

You would call him "Your Royal Highness" when talking
to him, and subsequently, "sir."

As for their son, he is:

> His Royal Highness
> The Prince Charles
> Prince of Wales
> His address

In talking to him, one addresses him as one does his father.

What about Princess Grace?

In writing to her, one addresses the envelope:

> Her Serene Highness,
> Princess Grace of Monaco
> Palace of Monaco

One addresses her as "Your Serene Highness," and subsequently "ma'am," and one refers to her and His Serene
Highness Prince Rainier as "Their Serene Highnesses."

*When a woman used to have an audience with the pope in
Rome, she wore a long black or navy dress, all covered up,
with a lace mantilla. What is the dress code I should observe
at present?*

Wear any conservative dress or suit. If you wore a décolleté dress or something like shorts, it would be considered
improper. You no longer have to wear a head covering. If
you are Catholic, and if it's a smaller audience with the Holy
Father, it is nice to wear a mantilla but not obligatory.

*Is there anything in particular I should remember when I
have dinner aboard a U.S. Navy aircraft carrier?*

Watch your smoking—it is not permitted in some areas of
the ship. Also, don't bring your host a present of liquor. (It's
against regulations to drink on board an official naval vessel.)
Also refer to the ship as she." Only small craft are "boats."

*I want to send a gift to the President at the White House—
and to his family. Is this permitted?*

The chances that the First Family will see your present are
slight. Each administration makes its own rules about sending
back automatically any "gift of value" (and a gift of value
may be anything from $25 to $50 and up). Also, food has
to be confiscated by the Secret Service to guard against
poisoning attempts, so anything made at home with loving
hands will never see anything but the trash can.

If I were you, I'd send them a letter or a greeting card.

*We have organized a new charity and are having our first
bona fide meeting of the board. What should I know about
parliamentary rules?*

Consult a book that's available in every public library:
Robert's Rules of Order. You can simplify the rules in this
standard reference text, but if you follow the basic ones,
you'll be running your meeting in a neat, orderly, and lawful
fashion.

Remember, the chairman has control of the meeting, and
should exert it. Anyone who wishes to speak must receive
permission from the chair first.

You can call your officers "chairperson" or whatever you
wish. I personally prefer to use "Madam Chairman," "Mr.
Chairman," "Madam President," and "Mr. President."

You in the Public Eye

The Art of Making Conversation

If you don't know someone and that person starts to talk to you, you don't have to answer, do you?

A thoughtful and kind person answers. It's impolite not to. All it takes to answer someone who begins chatting with you is a few impersonal comments. You don't have to give your life history, but if you speak with a pleasant voice, you are showing yourself to be a nice person.

Here's an example of an impolite and a polite answer to someone's observation about the weather, given when two strangers are standing next to each other in the supermarket checkout line:

"It sure is humid, isn't it? Maybe we're going to get that big rainstorm after all."
"Yes."

or

"It sure is humid, isn't it? Maybe we're going to get that big rainstorm after all."
"I hope so. The fields and the lawns are all so parched. We really need rain."

The second person is a nice human being; the first one is not.

What do you think it takes to be a good conversationalist?

Basic intelligence, a desire to please, and a sense of humor.

*Is part of being a good conversationalist knowing all the latest
"in" slang words and jargon fashionable in the jet set, and film
or TV society?*

Part of being a good conversationalist is that one doesn't
pepper one's language with slang—and never with bad language, either.

A good conversationalist has a good vocabulary—one that
is timeless rather than "faddish."

*I'm tongue-tied when I'm in a social group. I freeze up. Is
there any way I can become more at ease in conversation?*

You sound as if you don't have enough self-confidence.
Build up your confidence by becoming an expert in something—anything. Learn to talk amusingly and dramatically
about that subject.

Learn to read all the day's news events, too, and keep in
your mind the most important ones, so that when there is a
moment of total silence at a party, you can make a comment
about something in that day's news. Everyone around you will
be grateful that you broke the awkward silence.

Becoming at ease in making conversation is like consider-
ing yourself to be a handsome chest of drawers. Each drawer
is crammed full of a certain specialized topic or perhaps a
general topic on which you have something to say—because
you have read about it, or researched it, or heard others'
opinions and drawn conclusions from them.

Once you have all those drawers full, it's a question of
knowing which drawer to open at which moment. Once you've
learned the timing of conversational topics, you have learned
the art of it.

You don't, for example, when everyone has just finished
roaring with laughter at someone's story, introduce the fact
that a murder wiped out a family of eight, and did everyone
read about it?

When someone at the table has just been fired from his or
her corporation, you don't talk about the terrible hardships
the latest recession has wrought upon the middle class. You
don't, when everyone has finished dessert and has consumed
too much of everything, suddenly launch into the subject of
the strange mating habits of a Southeast Asian fly—that is,

unless you're so funny about it, you have the entire table convulsed in laughter.

Timing is everything in good conversation. When people look and sound as though they are low, it's time for you to bring them "up." People love to hear about international scandal, juicy gossip; if you have any, impart it, but never with the intent to harm, and make sure anything you say is already in the public domain, or about to become part of it.

When all else fails at the dinner table, come forth with a smashingly good comment about the host's or hostess's cooking. Your compliment will be appreciated, and it will spark a whole new line of conversation, probably gratefully welcomed by everyone seated at that table.

Public Speaking

I have to give a speech before a large group of people—my first. How do I go about preparing myself?

The first thing you do is to write a good speech. Without that, any other preparation is meaningless.

Be sure your speech has a beginning, middle, and end; that it has some humor in it, no matter how serious the subject; that it gets one or more specific points across; and that it is not too complicated or couched in too-technical language.

Make it brief. If you are the only speaker at a luncheon, for example, speak for fifteen to twenty minutes. If you are one of several speakers on a crowded program, talk no more than five minutes.

Practice your speech over and over. Tape yourself and notice if your voice, diction, and delivery improve with each taping. The more you practice, the less time you will have to spend looking at your text, and the more time you can look out at the audience. Give your speech to an audience of yourself—as you face a mirror.

How do I know if I have a pleasant voice?

If someone tapes your presentation, you can tell by listening hard. Work on a speech tone that is neither too loud nor too soft, too high or too low. Weed out the repetitious "uh, uh . . ." that may be in your delivery.

If you have definite voice problems and are in a position in your business or in your community life where a good voice is a necessary asset, work with a speech therapist or a voice coach. It will help your presentation—and your self-confidence.

What are the main things to remember when introducing the main speaker?

Put enthusiasm and pep into your voice. Make the audience full of expectations about the speaker. Give a short introduction. (Do not sound, however, as though you were reading the speaker's *Who's Who* entry from the book.)

What are the duties of a master of ceremonies?

The master of ceremonies should introduce everyone deftly, should inject some humor into the proceedings when things are dull, and should move the program right along, so that the guests can leave the hall or ballroom or wherever the event is held without having had time to be bored.

The M.C. has to handle disasters (such as the microphones not working properly); it's his or her responsibility to interrupt a speaker who goes on too long with a note which says, "Please finish your talk. There is *no* more time!"

I often have to speak in front of small to medium-size groups. My hands shake every time, and I can hear the papers rattle as I hold them. Is there any way to get over this?

One way is to leave your papers in a notebook or on a clipboard where you can't pick them up. You should leave them untouched on the lectern, and if you must do something with your hands, grip the two sides of the lectern.

How should the speaker of the evening be dressed?

Very well. All eyes are on the speaker, so he or she should be conservatively dressed, fashionably dressed, and meticulously groomed. "Fashionably dressed" when applied to a speaker does not mean that he or she has to be garbed in an Italian- or French-designer original; but it means that the necktie on the man is the proper width for the times, that the woman's hemline is right for the fashions of the day. The speaker is very conspicuous, and if he or she is garishly, inappropriately, or sloppily dressed, no one will listen to the speech.

I'm in charge of handling the celebrity speakers who are coming to our town hall this year. Is there anything special I should remember?

Send the speaker the full schedule you have planned. Don't spring any press interviews or TV appearances you haven't talked over with the speaker beforehand and received permission to book.

Explain to the speaker in your letter the nature of the group that is sponsoring the lecture.

Arrange for emergency pressing in the hotel or motel, if it is necessary. Ask a woman speaker well ahead if she will need a hairdresser's appointment on the day of the talk.

Don't take the celebrity home to your family to "have a chat." That's the last thing he or she wants to do. Don't pepper him or her with questions relating to his past life or achievements. Don't make him give his speech just for you ahead of time.

Don't give a woman speaker a corsage—send flowers to her home instead.

Don't give the speaker something heavy and impossible to pack, like a large plaque or paperweight with your organization's logo on it. It will go into the first available trash can, so don't waste your money and the speaker's packing space.

Don't make the speaker sign autographs for every member of your family and every friend you ever had. A couple of special dedications are enough.

Restaurant Dining

If someone asks you to dinner, shouldn't he make the reservation, tell you where to come, and pay for the meal?

Yes. The person who does the asking takes the responsibility for making the arrangements—and for paying, unless it is clearly understood beforehand that it is "dutch."

What do you do if you think you've been invited to a restaurant, so you don't bring any money and then you're suddenly confronted with having to pay half the bill?

You must pay your share of the bill in this circumstance. It happens often in our lives, simply because we don't pay enough attention to communicating and preplanning our engagements. We should all be specific about when, where, and who pays, when dates and arrangements are jointly made.

If you're in a restaurant with no money in a situation like this, go to the captain and tell him your plight and that you will send the money tomorrow—by messenger. If you show identification and if you sign a receipt for money owed, you might be able to arrange for payment of your share tomorrow. Otherwise, you are going to have to borrow money from your friends at the table. It is embarrassing, but come up with a logical excuse for not having money or a credit card.

If you're giving a party in a restaurant, should you await your guests in the entrance of the restaurant, or should you go to the table?

If the entrance is tiny, there really isn't room for you to congregate all your guests there. It's better in this case to go straight to your table.

However, remember to arrive *before* your guests do. It's extremely rude for the hosts to arrive after their guests!

If I'm awaiting my host in the restaurant and he or she is very late, is it all right for me to order my own drink at the bar and pay for it?

It's far nicer to wait for your host to arrive before ordering a drink.

How long should you wait for a "no-show" in a restaurant before leaving? Do you tip the waiter who brought you water

*and bread or perhaps a drink while you were waiting end-
lessly?*

When someone is twenty minutes late, go and call that person's office or home to find out what happened. If you can't
get through to your tardy guest's office or home, wait for
thirty minutes in all, and then leave the restaurant.

Yes, you should tip the table waiter for the water, rolls,
and attention, over and above the price of the drink you may
have ordered.

*When you take guests to a restaurant, how do you seat them
when there's a banquette involved?*

You, the host, should give your guests the banquette seats
(which are the best ones, since they view the restaurant and
the other diners). Anyone from out of town should have
priority on these seats. If you are a foursome of old friends,
the polite thing to do is to let the two women sit on the ban-
quettes, with the men opposite.

If it's a business dinner of men and women, you would
seat men and women next to each other on the banquette
(your clients and customers or your potential clients and
customers). You and your spouse or associates in the business
would take the facing seats. You would arrange the seating
so that men and women have alternating seats—or across
from each other.

Does a man order for his woman companion?

He asks her what she wants, and he orders for her if it
makes the ordering more efficient. He should never order anything for her without her expressly having requested it.

Men today who are increasingly aware of the women in
their businesses who wish to be treated like colleagues instead
of helpless creatures, allow the women at the table to order
for themselves.

*What if you are dining in a restaurant as someone's guest and
you are longing for a glass of wine? Is it all right to order it
if no one else had one?*

If your host, for one reason or another, does not order wine for your table, you are better off leaving the subject untouched. It might embarrass the person to realize the wine was forgotten, or perhaps that he couldn't afford to order it.

When you desire service at your table, how do you call for it?

If a man is serving you and he is within earshot, call out "Waiter" softly (or "Waitress" if a woman is doing the honors). Do the summoning with a pleasant tone of voice, not like a sergeant barking orders in a boot camp. If the waiter or waitress is already occupied taking someone's order, wait patiently before interrupting that person's time at the other table.

Is it all right to ask for a doggie bag from the waiter if one is unable to eat a particular wonderful piece of meat or dessert, for example?

In a restaurant, it's all right (but not in a private home). If the staff in the restaurant is frantically busy, without enough people to handle the job, don't ask for a doggie bag; it is an imposition in such a case.

Why do some restaurants require a jacket and tie for men or prohibit jeans for women? After all, if one is neat and clean —or in designer jeans—one should be allowed to eat in a public place.

Expensive restaurants are able to charge those prices partly because of the quality of the food that is served, and the quality of the service, but also because of the nature of the atmosphere. If a restaurant has a luxurious ambience, it is completely shattered by someone who arrives too casually dressed. If people have made an effort to look their most attractive best, their spirit of festiveness can be broken if others look as though they've been walking through the woods.

Dressing up for an expensive restaurant is as much a question of being considerate of the other patrons as it is of assuring you and your friends an attractive scene to gaze upon during the meal.

Is it all right if you're trying out all the famous dishes in a certain restaurant for everyone to order different things and then give everyone else a taste?

Yes, provided the different portions given to others at the table are not meted out from an already used plate or with an already used fork or spoon.

Arrange in advance to have the waiter bring each person an extra little plate onto which each of you spoons with a clean utensil a bit of this and a bit of that. Otherwise it looks sloppy—and somewhat unsanitary.

Aren't people who never order dessert (and who pooh-pooh others who do) awfully rude when they lean over to "have a taste"?

Yes, they are. Constant "tasters" are a big bore for everyone. If they want to taste something so badly, they should order it for themselves.

When you're eating in a coffee shop or at a drugstore counter, what are you supposed to do with the paper containers you used for mustard, sugar, and things like that?

It's nice to fold them neatly and deposit them in the ashtray, if it's not being used. Otherwise, one may deposit them on the saucer of the coffeecup or under the rim of a plate.

I was always taught that when a man who is not "loaded" takes a woman to a restaurant, his date should order very lightly. Is this true today?

Yes, and it's equally true if a woman is footing the bill for a male guest. It's just basic good manners when you're someone's guest to order modestly. If your host insists you have something grander, and says he or she is "going to have the fillet of beef" this evening, you as the guest may certainly follow suit.

If the guest orders first, it's nice to go easy, if one doesn't know the personal situation of the host.

A person in business is severely called to task if the expense accounts are too high, so don't think that just because you're the guest of some corporation too much lavishness won't be criticized.

Tipping

If you're at a very posh restaurant and you're confronted with a maître d'hôtel, captain, wine steward, and waiter, what in heaven's name do you give in tips?

A "posh restaurant" requires no less than 20 percent, but it usually ends up being more. If you're in a less expensive restaurant, 15 to 18 percent is the usual tip.

In a very fine restaurant, add 20 percent on to the bill or the credit-card slip, but then divide the 20 percent into a major share for the waiter, and a lesser share for the captain.

For example, a dinner for two might cost $100 in a luxury spot. Twenty percent of $100 is $20, so you would give $15 to the waiter and $5 to the captain. If a wine steward served you (a sommelier), you would give him $3 for your bottle of wine. On your way out, you would give the headwaiter anywhere from one to five dollars, depending on how much attention he gave you. Then the coatroom person would receive another $1. The man out in front who gets your cab receives another $1.

A "simple" dinner for two has therefore cost at least $126.

In a more modest location, the total will be, thankfully, less.

You and Someone Who Is Ill

Do sick people want visitors in their hospital rooms, or does it make them feel worse? I never know whether to go or not to go.

Always offer to go. If the patient is too ill to see you, it will be communicated to you, but the fact that you care enough about the person to take the time and trouble to go to the hospital is greatly appreciated. As for the terminally ill, they are often abandoned by their friends, and this is cruel beyond belief.

Do you send a get-well card to someone who is not going to get better? What do you do?

You don't send a Get-Well or any of those cheerful, humorous cards relating to someone's ailment. You can send a friendship card—like a scene of a beautiful flower garden, with a message inside, "Thinking of you"—with your own written words added on the card.

What are some good gifts for people in the hospital?

Easy-to-care-for plants; a gift certificate for two to a good restaurant the hospitalized person can use when he or she is well again; an exciting book for someone who is getting well; an amusing, easy-to-read, or else beautiful picture book for someone who is quite sick; a tape or cassette on which you and your family or your mutual friends or office associates have recorded all the news; some wonderful-smelling soap, cologne, or talcum—anything to make the patient and the surroundings touched with a delightful fragrance; notepaper for the patient who is almost well again to use when writing thank-you notes for all the gifts and flowers sent; fashion magazines for the patient who's interested in clothes; sports-car magazines for the person interested in cars; science magazines for the lover of science. And for the person confined for a long time in the hospital, the friend who organizes some of the other friends to go in on the purchase of a good-quality dressing gown, nightgown, or pajamas—that's a friend indeed.

When you're sitting by the bed of someone who's really sick, are you supposed to be a cheerful, bubbling chatterbox all the time? Are you supposed to ignore the other person's illness?

No. You should let the other person know that "it must be very tough, very hard, what you're going through."

Let the person who is ill take the lead. He or she may need desperately to talk about being ill at that time. There

may be complaints to air, a need to gather sympathy. There
may be a fear of dying to articulate.

Follow the lead of the person you are visiting. If he or she
insists on talking about the outside world, of which you are
part, then talk about it. Talk about the cheerful side of the
outside world, however, not the depressing.

*When you visit someone in the hospital, how long should you
stay? I always feel torn. I feel my friend wants me to stay
and talk, yet I can see she is tired.*

If your friend is very sick, stay only from five to ten minutes. If you're visiting someone who is not seriously ill, stay
from ten to fifteen minutes. No matter what the condition of
that patient may be, a visit from anyone is tiring to a hospitalized person. Leave on time, even if you are urged to
"stay a little more."

*I have a friend dying of cancer. I can't bear to touch her.
This worries me, and makes me feel that I'm not a real
friend.*

Take her hand and hold it in yours. You don't have to kiss
her, but if you can, do it. Someone who is dying needs every
ounce of reassurance a friend can give. If you stay at the
other end of the bed, you are making your friend's agony
worse—the agony of leaving, of separation, of not being able
to hold on to this life.

*If the hospitalized friend I'm visiting is smoking, it's all right
for me to smoke, isn't it?*

No, even if the patient is smoking, even if the doctor is
smoking, or if another patient in the room is smoking, it
doesn't matter. It's bad manners and very unhealthy to add
to the smoke in anyone's hospital room.

*I become angry at the indifference of the nurses. They won't
tell me about the condition of my friend in the hospital.*

They are not indifferent. They are not allowed to tell you about the patient's condition. You must ask the doctor, instead of giving the nurse the third degree.

Traveling

When you're traveling by air, isn't it more efficient to bring your suitcase and other items into the cabin, thus avoiding the interminable delays in the baggage area of the airport of destination?

You may feel it's more efficient for you, but if you bring all your baggage into the cabin, it makes life impossible for the flight attendants and for the people sitting beside you.

People who board with lots of totes, packages, dress bags, and shopping bags are causing a safety hazard (according to federal regulations, everything must be properly stowed for takeoff and landing). For other passengers, having to step over (and trip over) someone's personal possessions hogging the precious space around the passengers' feet is really aggravating.

Bring aboard only one item—something that will fit easily beneath the seat in front of you, and check everything else. If you're bringing a suit bag, make it a three-suiter, not a larger one. There simply isn't room to accommodate giant bags in small aircraft closets.

Someone told me it's rude to bring on your own food to eat on a short flight when a meal isn't being served. Why?

Because passengers are jammed into airplanes, and your neighbors in such close proximity do not appreciate the sound of your munching, or the smell of your food—an eating experience they are not sharing.

What is the proper term for the personnel who serve you on an airplane?

"Flight attendants." The terms "hostess" and "stewardess" are passé, because there are many men involved in this career today.

What if the person next to you is a chatterbox and you don't want to talk?

Smile and say very nicely, "I'm sorry. I wish I could talk, but I have some work that has to be finished before we land." If you're holding a book or a magazine, explain that "I have to finish this for some research I'm doing."

If you have very long legs and the person in front of you reclines the seat, is it all right to tell that person it's bothering you?

Yes, but do it graciously. "I hope you don't mind, but when you put your seat back, it cuts right into my knees and stops the circulation. I'm too long-legged, you see."

Ninety-nine percent of the people in this world will accept that and will put their seats forward. If you have one of the one-percent group, the only thing you can do is change seats with someone else who is shorter.

How can you show your appreciation to a flight crew that did an extra special job? Some quiet tipping perhaps?

No, one never tips any part of the crew. Tell them verbally how much you appreciated their professional service, and tell the flight crew what a nice flight it was. If you want to go beyond that, write to the president of the airline and commend the crew. Any such recommendation goes into their files and may be very useful to them.

What should one do to organize for foreign travel?

The first thing to do is to be sure your passport is up-to-date, with visas for any countries requiring them, and with the proper inoculations required for certain countries.

Order a plentiful supply of any medications you need.

Type several copies of your complete schedule, and leave a copy with whoever needs it (your baby-sitter, your office, your lawyer).

Assemble all the camera equipment and film you'll need—in many places you won't be able to find what you use.

Pack an extra pair or two of glasses, if you wear them.

Get traveler's checks from a local bank.

Bring your own toilet articles—a good supply—and pack your own soap. Hotel soap often leaves a great deal to be desired.

Be prepared for rain.

Pack a small traveling alarm clock—and a strong light bulb if you're an in-bed reader.

Leave your good jewelry at home.

If you're going to another country, don't pack electrical gadgets.

Isn't it all right to take things from a hotel—like a towel—as a souvenir?

No, because that's not souvenir-collecting, that's hotel-robbing.

Being a Good American

When our national anthem is played, what are we supposed to do?

If you are in a public place, you should rise promptly and stand quietly at attention. (The old and infirm do not have to rise.) If people are asked to sing it, everyone who can should. (many people can't reach the high notes). A man wearing a hat should remove it and hold it with his right hand over his heart. Others might wish to stand with their hands over their hearts.

Our national anthem is four stanzas long, but the second and third stanzas are usually omitted. The first and the fourth are the ones most often sung, but usually only the first stanza is sung.

I've noticed when foreign personages or teams are here in this country, their anthems are sung first. Why?

Simply as a mark of courtesy to them. When an American team is abroad playing another country's or when our statesmen make an official visit to another country, "The Star-Spangled Banner" is always played first.

When I'm in another country and I happen to know their national anthem, is it unpatriotic of me to sing it?

No, and if you learn their anthem and sing it properly, you are pleasing them very much. It is a courtesy to the country you are visiting.

Meeting People

When you're sitting having cocktails in someone's home, isn't it true that a man stands up to greet new arrivals but that a woman remains seated and smiles her hello?

No, a woman should rise to greet anyone new, as well as a man. This is what equality is all about—equality of opportunity means equality of manners, too, and the same amount of effort put into human relations.

Do you have to shake hands when you meet someone new? What about when you meet someone you already know?

No matter where you are or how well you know someone, the nice, warm way to say hello to a person is to step forward, smile, and extend your hand for a handshake. This human contact of one hand with another is an all-important symbolic physical gesture. Really good friends may combine that handshake with a pat on the other person's arm; two women may kiss on the cheeks; a man and a woman may kiss on the cheeks if they haven't seen each other for a long time.

But what about people who have just seen each other, then run into each other at a party and kiss each other again on the cheek?

It's redundant and rather silly. A firm handshake is much more meaningful—and graceful—than a random sideswiping of cheeks.

If you meet in the street, it's cold, and you're wearing gloves, you shake hands with your gloves on, don't you?

It's much nicer to remove the glove from your shaking hand, even if it is cold. People would rather feel someone's hand in a handshake than a piece of leather or fabric.

I'm always forgetting people's names. It's very embarrassing, because I forget good friends' names as well as new acquaintances'. What does one do in introductions when this happens?

If you can remember either the first or the last name, come forth with that. For example, let's say you and your husband meet two acquaintances of yours on the street, neither of whom has met your husband before. You remember the given name of one person and the married name of the other. Just bluff it.

"Susan, I want my husband to meet you. Bob, this is Susan. And Mrs. Williams, at last I can introduce my husband to you. Mrs. Williams, Bob Jones." In all likelihood, neither woman will notice you did not know her full name.

If you can't remember any name at all, talk fast in a flattering build-up of the other person—and the other person won't even realize you never mentioned his or her name.

"Bob, I've talked about this fantastic woman to you many times. She is the number-one volunteer at our Church Council. The Council would not survive without her. She has organized entire neighborhoods, raised twice as much money for the church as has ever been raised before. She's terrific!"

By the time you have finished, Mrs. What's-her-name feels like a million dollars, thanks to your nice comments, and she and your husband start talking to each other without realizing her name was never mentioned.

If you forget your best friend's name in trying to introduce her, toss it off with a laugh. Everyone has those momentary lapses, and if you just chuckle over it, people will relax, smile, and forget it.

Others become embarrassed when you become embarrassed about something. If you act as though you think it's funny, they will, too.

I think one of the rudest things a person can do is to be talking to someone else and to ignore you when you come up to say hello. Shouldn't people try to introduce the person they are with to the person who comes up to say hello?

Yes, when two or more are talking and a friend of one of the group approaches, that friend should not only be introduced to the rest of the group but also be brought into their conversation while standing there. It is very inconsiderate to exclude anyone from a conversation. For the person who has been excluded, there is only one course of action: departure!

Smoking Etiquette

Is a man supposed to light a woman's cigarette in the evening? I know he's not supposed to in the office, but what about at night, in a purely social situation?

No, a man does not have to light a woman's cigarette in the evening or at any time. Since smoking is a death warrant for some people, it is no longer considered good manners to help someone sign that warrant.

Does this mean hosts don't have to provide cigarettes at their parties anymore?

Exactly. They should, however, provide ashtrays and matches for their guests who do smoke.

I'm an incurable chain smoker, and I die if I don't have a cigarette in my hand. If there are no ashtrays on the desk of someone with whom I have an appointment, is it all right if I ask, "Do you mind if I smoke?"

No, if there is no ashtray on the desk of the person you are visiting, you really should not ask to smoke. (Have a cigarette

in the rest room before the appointment.) You may "die" if
you don't have a cigarette in your hand, but other people feel
they should not have to die from inhaling the smoke of that
cigarette in your hand.

*What do you do if you have just ordered a wonderful (and
expensive) dinner in a fine restaurant, and the man on the
banquette next to you lights up his pipe or cigar?*

Speak quietly to the headwaiter about it. If he's a good
headwaiter, he will politely ask the smoker to cease and de-
sist. If he can't or won't cope with it, he should at least try to
find you another table, far from the offending smoke stream.

If the headwaiter fails to do even that, ask for your bill for
the food you have eaten so far, and leave the restaurant. That
place will have a large blackball as far as you and your friends
are concerned.

*If someone is smoking on an elevator—and of course, it's
against the law—is it all right to say something to that person?*

I for one believe that one *should* say something, but you
don't want a confrontation in an elevator. Wait until your
elevator is discharging everyone, and tell the person in a nice
voice that "Smoking in an elevator is against the law, you
know. It's such a small space, there isn't enough air to
breathe."

A person who acts in an antisocial and unacceptable manner needs to have someone tell him or her not to do it. Otherwise, he or she will continue to do it without a second
thought.

If you get your message across in a nice tone, without
hostility, you might teach that person some manners.

*Is it all right to put a sign on one's desk in the office, and
also in the living room of one's home, asking people not to
smoke?*

I think it's fine on a desk, but not so nice in your home.
As for the desk signs, the one I like the best so far is from
the American Cancer Society: THANK YOU FOR NOT SMOKING.

I have become more and more allergic to smoke, and have stayed away from entertaining for that reason. Now I feel I have the right to have guests and to forbid them to smoke in my house. Is that considered proper?

"Forbid" is a strong word. Tell them on the telephone when you invite them that you have become very allergic to smoke and that you want your home to remain smoke-free. Add that you'll understand if any smoking guests absent themselves from the group periodically to go out-of-doors, if they must, to smoke.

If you fully warn them of the situation in advance, you are giving them the option of accepting your invitation and abiding by the rules, or of regretting your invitation. Never spring on your guests an edict of "No Smoking Whatsoever."

Isn't it all right to smoke during the meal, if your hosts say they don't mind?

The other people around you at the table may mind very much. Your hosts may mind very much, too, but are too polite to tell you. Smoke wafting into a person's nostrils when he or she is eating tends to ruin the ability to appreciate the taste and the nuances of the cuisine.

No one should light up a cigarette until the dessert is finished and coffee is being served.

I am a constant smoker and I usually eat at a lunch counter every day. I really want and enjoy that one cigarette with my coffee. Is it so terrible of me to smoke at this point?

Turn to the person on your left and your right and ask very nicely, "Would it bother you if I smoked a cigarette now?"

Usually, when a smoker is that polite, the person who minds the smoke says, "That's all right," just because the smoker was so apologetic about it.

If you have your neighbors' permission to smoke, watch the smoke very carefully from your cigarette. Make sure the air-conditioning vent is not forcing it into someone's eyes or nose. Watch it constantly, so that if anyone is getting the full impact of your smoke, it's *you.*

What if the person next to you is smoking at the counter, and that smoke is bothering you?

Turn to the person in a very polite, gracious way: "Your cigarette smoke is blowing my way. If you don't mind . . ." The smoker will usually put out the cigarette at once. If the smoker doesn't, move away. You don't want to sit next to that objectionable person anyway. Life is too short.

If a man looks okay walking down the street with a cigarette in his lips, shouldn't it be okay for a woman to do it?

It is unattractive for a man *or* a woman to smoke on the street.

The Appropriateness of Dress

If you don't know what to wear to a party, what do you do? Is it better to overdress or underdress?

The first thing you do when you don't know what to wear to a party is to call your hosts and ask how "everyone is going to dress." They will tell you how *they*, the hosts, are going to dress, and you can follow suit.

As for overdressing or underdressing, the rule of thumb always is: the simpler, the better; the more understated, the more elegant; the less decorated, the more noticeable.

If you're at a black-tie party and you didn't know people were supposed to dress formally, what should you do? Stay or go home to change?

If you live close by, go home and change. You'll feel more comfortable. If you live far away, apologize to your hosts, say you made a careless error in forgetting it was black-tie (never admit you didn't know what "Black Tie" meant on the invitation), and laugh about it with strangers whom you meet at the party. Explain that you're "so busy, you've become absentminded."

Isn't it a host's duty to make a guest feel comfortable wearing whatever he or she has put on? Isn't that both polite and considerate?

Yes, but that does not take into account the state of misery into which the wrongly dressed guest might be thrown. If the person is really upset about how he or she is dressed, there is only one remedy: if "home" is nearby, one should go home to change. The host should understand that.

What's the rule about wearing jewelry? I believe a woman should wear what she has—show it off—instead of keeping jewels in a bank vault.

There are two reasons for being careful about wearing an overload of jewels. The first involves security, the chance that wearing too many jewels invites instant robbery; the second reason concerns taste. Jewelry should be worn sparingly, to set off the various pieces in their own beautiful setting. Otherwise, too much jewelry makes a woman look as though she were modeling costume jewelry for a junk shop.

Is it all right for a woman to wear pants to church?

Most clergymen would rather have her attend services in pants than not come at all. However, a woman in church looks more appropriately and conservatively dressed if she is wearing a skirt.

Are gloves the sign of a "lady"?

They aren't thought of in that context today. However, they *are* thought of as being necessary in winter—protective of delicate skin. The right gloves are also a "perfect finishing touch" to a woman's outfit.

If you're wearing long white gloves at some very formal affair, what do you do with them when you're eating?

Roll back the gloves at the wrist, if you are wearing that kind of long white glove. If not, remove your white gloves for eating.

Are you supposed to wear the bracelet outside the glove or inside?

Many women of fashion and taste say that bracelets should not be a part of a gloved hand, unless they can be worn at the top of the glove.

When a man insists on wearing a bow tie when bow ties are not in fashion, isn't he making an embarrassing mistake?

Not necessarily. Some distinguished, well-dressed men cling to the same fashion all their lives, but they have a certain sense of their own style, they are meticulously groomed, and they always look "right."

Women's magazines are always informing us of the fashion mistakes women make. Men often don't know about the ones they make, nor do they read about them.

The same number of men and women are unable to look coldly and clinically at themselves in a mirror, to recognize their mistakes. Often, a diplomatic friend has to do the job. When a man north of the Mason-Dixon line wears white shoes to business after Labor Day, someone should tip him off. If he wears white socks to work, someone should tip him off, too, unless he is in Bermuda, wearing Bermuda shorts and long white knee socks!

Is it all right for women to wear shorts in the city?

No, a woman going to work or a woman who is a mature person should not wear shorts in city streets. If she's on her way to a tennis game, a light coat as a cover-up should make her feel more comfortable.

What is your definition of a "mature woman" in terms of fashion?

My definition of "mature" is someone who is at least eighteen years old in terms of experience and attitudes toward life.

Does the woman who dresses sexily on the job know just what she's doing?

She may not. But she should soon know when job promotions never seem to materialize.

Are hats considered part of the well-dressed man's and woman's wardrobes today?

Hats used to be a necessity in a person's wardrobe. Today, they are not seen as often—but when they are worn by someone who finishes the "look" of his or her costume, they are suddenly essential again.

In other words, a really elegant-looking person can owe part of the success of his or her appearance to the hat on his or her head!

A Short Guide to Appropriate Gifts

The Philosophy of Giving

I love to give people presents, but hardly ever receive any in return. I keep on doing it, but others ask me why.

You enjoy the act of giving. There is pleasure in this, and it's what giving is all about. A person of wealth who "lets someone else" on the staff order the gift, write the card, and dispatch the present never enjoys the act of giving, nor does that gift ever have any meaning, other than its monetary value.

What is the real secret to knowing exactly what to give someone?

There are several points to consider in selecting a gift for someone. First, there may be a need. The recipient may need something very badly, and this requirement should be taken care of first. If a young couple about to be married can't afford a car, but must have a car, your financial contribution toward that car, however small, is the present you should give.

Let's say the person for whom you are selecting a gift has a great interest or a hobby. If your present is directed in that way, you are going to be successful as a gift-giver.

Let's say you accidentally stumble across something you know would please someone else. You have a friend who loves things with hearts on them, and you see a scarf printed with little red hearts. You buy it and save it for her as a holiday gift. Or you pass by a shop selling old maps when

248

you're on a business trip. You find one of the town where your map-collecting friend was born. You buy it and give it to him on his birthday.

Being creative about what you give someone is important, and it adds to the pleasure of the act for the donor and for the recipient.

Presents for Children

As a godparent, I want to give my godchild a present other than the traditional silver mug or fork-and-spoon set, because the baby has them already. Any ideas for a baby gift?

Why not present baby with its first book? A fine edition of a great classic? If you can afford it, have the book bound in leather and put the baby's name, birthday, and "First Book" gold-tooled on the cover.

Or open a savings account in the baby's name with a $25 or $50 deposit. (First you have to have the parents obtain a Social Security number for the baby.) Give the parents the passbook, when it's ready, wrapped as a gift.

If you work for a company listed on an exchange, what about the gift of a share of stock?

If you're an excellent amateur photographer, how about donating your services to record the baby's christening party —giving the family a photo album with the pictures nicely placed inside?

I never know what to give as an infant present.

Toys for the bathtub, delightful mobiles to hang over the crib, and colorful rubber teething toys are always useful and enjoyable for the baby and the parents.

What about the toddler?

Books, with large illustrations, or with pop-ups, or something with textured interest, to help the baby begin a lifetime of loving books, as well as help the adults enjoy reading to the baby. And, of course, soft, squeezable, huggable, *safe* stuffed animals are always a success.

What about the child who has just begun school?

Blocks and building toys are good for the development of these young people's coordination. Other possibilities are: puppets they can put on their hands and fantasize with; small blackboards, chalk, and erasers to encourage them to draw or write; paint sets to make them love to practice art; and books that teach them in an amusing way numbers and the alphabet.

Presents for Graduates

What kind of a present is certain to be a success with a graduating eighth-grader?

A suitcase to use for overnights, camping, or vacations; cash; a dictionary; sports equipment according to his or her great interest; a gift certificate to a shop selling records, cassettes, and tapes; a magazine subscription to a publication that deals with the student's favorite hobby or interest; a trip for the student and a parent to a place of great historical importance—like Washington, D.C., Williamsburg, or Boston.

What about the high-school graduate?

Again, luggage, needed for college; a portable electric typewriter; world atlas; subscription to the student's hometown newspaper; photo album and rolls of film to record the college experience; clock radio; electric hair dryer.

What should one give to a college graduate?

Since most college graduates leave home and establish their own homes as they begin their jobs and careers, any help toward furnishing them with the basic necessities is enthusiastically welcomed. Do some research. Maybe it's a toaster that's needed, or a share in buying a color TV set.

A gift of money or a gift certificate to a major department store is always good. So is something for the new business career: an attaché case (or briefcase), a good pen-and-pencil set, a nice frame, a leather engagement book (replaceable pages).

Christmas and Hanukkah

I am very disorganized about my Christmas list, and wish there was some prescribed system that would help me.

If you keep a separate file for each year's holiday giving, it will help you the next year. Put down the person's name and what you gave, or list the nonprofit organization and what you gave to it. You might make major subheadings, and list the individuals within each group. Examples of subheads:

1. Immediate family.
2. Peripheral family (in-laws, cousins, nieces and nephews, godchildren).
3. If you live in an apartment building with service, cash is usually given to the superintendent, doormen, service-car operator, etc.
4. Personal-service people involved in your life: your clergyman, pediatrician, doctor, dentist, hairdresser, mail carriers, parcel-post deliverymen, newspaper-delivery people, housekeeper, baby-sitter, etc.
5. As an office executive, you should remember your personal secretary with a small, impersonal gift.
6. Don't forget those charitable contributions in the holiday season.

What if someone sends you a Christmas gift and you never even thought of giving that person something? Should you rush down to a store and send a gift?

No, write a gracious, warm thank-you note, but make no reference to the fact you did not send a gift. You may have done something nice for that person, and it's that person's way of saying thank you. Do not feel obligated when someone you don't know very well sends you something.

When do you know that a gift is inappropriate—a bribe, in a way?

When someone who is not a good personal friend sends you an expensive gift in the hopes you will bring your influence to bear in a business deal, the only action to take is to return the gift at once, with a note saying, "Thank you for your nice thought, but I cannot accept such a present."

What do you do when you're really broke and can't send any presents for the holidays?

Write a personal letter to each relative and friend who would have received a gift, saying something like, "There won't be any presents from me this year, but there is a billion dollars' worth of good wishes for the holiday season sent with this note."

If you're good with your hands, you can, of course, make something (like a key ring with the person's monogram needlepointed on the tag, or a painting of the recipient's house, or a specially designed telephone-book cover).

If you're a cook, you can deliver a freshly made casserole or box of cookies beautifully wrapped as a present.

Is giving a gift certificate the lazy person's way out?

Not at all. It may be one of the most creative gifts the recipient ever received in his or her life. A modern young couple, with an embryonic collection of fine old books would love nothing more than a gift certificate to a reputable dealer in old books—to pick out something themselves, to put their "collector's talents" into action. A tired woman executive would love nothing more than a gift certificate to a first-class health spa for women. An amateur wine connoisseur would enjoy a gift certificate to a wine dealer—to pick out his or her own very private choices. A young woman who has a very modest gift certificate may be able to buy a useless, luxurious thing—like sequin-patterned black hosiery for evening—just because the certificate will pay for it.

People love gift certificates. They are not cold, imagination-less gifts. What the donor *should* be creative about is the store or the company to which the certificate is assigned.

Index

ABOUT THE AUTHOR

LETITIA BALDRIGE began her career as Social Secretary to Ambassador and Mrs. David Bruce at the American Embassy in Paris. She was assistant to Ambassador Clare Boothe Luce at the American Embassy in Rome, and was the first Director of Public Relations for Tiffany & Co., the New York jeweler, as well as their first woman executive. In the early 1960s, she was called to Washington by President John F. Kennedy to serve as Social Secretary to the White House, as well as head of Mrs. Kennedy's secretariat. Along with supervising all social activities at the executive mansion, she handled Mrs. Kennedy's public relations, accompanied the Kennedys on all state visits abroad, and served on the Presidential advance team that makes all scheduling and protocol arrangements for those visits.

Ms. Baldrige was the first Director of Consumer Affairs for Burlington Industries, Inc., the world's largest textile company. She has headed her own public relations and marketing consulting firm, Letitia Baldrige Enterprises, Inc., since 1964.

She has written six books, contributes to magazines on a regular basis and writes a nationally syndicated column, "Contemporary Living" for the *Los Angeles Times* Syndicate. She has most recently published *Letitia Baldrige's Complete Guide to Executive Manners.*

Ms. Baldrige is married to real estate executive Robert Hollensteiner. They have two children and reside in Manhattan.

We Deliver!
And So Do These Bestsellers.

THE LATEST IN BOOKS
AND AUDIO CASSETTES

Paperbacks

❏	28354-5	SEDUCTION Amanda Quick	$5.99
❏	28594-7	SURRENDER Amanda Quick	$5.99
❏	29316-8	RAVISHED Amanda Quick	$4.99
❏	28435-5	A WORLD OF DIFFERENCE Leona Blair	$5.95
❏	28416-9	RIGHTFULLY MINE Doris Mortman	$6.50
❏	27032-X	FIRST BORN Doris Mortman	$5.99
❏	27283-7	BRAZEN VIRTUE Nora Roberts	$4.99
❏	27891-6	PEOPLE LIKE US Dominick Dunne	$5.99
❏	27260-8	WILD SWAN Celeste De Blasis	$5.95
❏	25692-0	SWAN'S CHANCE Celeste De Blasis	$5.95
❏	27790-1	A WOMAN OF SUBSTANCE	
		Barbara Taylor Bradford	$6.99
❏	29761-9	THE WILD ROSE Doris Mortman	$5.99
❏	28734-6	WELL-SCHOOLED IN MURDER	
		Elizabeth George	$5.99

Audio

❏	SEPTEMBER by Rosamunde Pilcher		
	Performance by Lynn Redgrave		
	180 Mins. Double Cassette	45241-X	$15.99
❏	THE SHELL SEEKERS by Rosamunde Pilcher		
	Performance by Lynn Redgrave		
	180 Mins. Double Cassette	45183-9	$15.99
❏	COLD SASSY TREE by Olive Ann Burns		
	Performance by Richard Thomas		
	180 Mins. Double Cassette	45166-9	$15.99
❏	WELL-SCHOOLED IN MURDER by Elizabeth George		
	Performance by Derek Jacobi		
	180 Mins. Double Cassette	45278-9	$15.99

Available at your local bookstore or use this page to order.

Send to: Bantam Books, Dept. FBS
          2451 S. Wolf Road
          Des Plaines, IL 60018

Please send me the items I have checked above. I am enclosing
$_____ (please add $2.50 to cover postage and handling). Send
check or money order, no cash or C.O.D.'s, please.

Mr./Ms._____

Address_____

City/State_____ Zip_____

Please allow four to six weeks for delivery.
Prices and availability subject to change without notice.   FBS 12/93